ANDEL

THE MEXICAN-KIOWA

CAPTIVE

ANDELE

The Mexican-Kiowa Captive

———

A Story of Real Life Among the Indians

J.J. Methvin

Introduction by James F. Brooks

University of New Mexico Press
Albuquerque

Library of Congress Cataloging-in-Publication Data
Methvin, J. J.
[Andele, or, The Mexican-Kiowa captive]
Andele, the Mexican-Kiowa captive: a story of real life among the
Indians / J. J. Methvin.—1st University of New Mexico Press
paperbound ed. / Introduction by James F. Brooks.
p.   cm.
Originally published: Andele, or, The Mexican-Kiowa captive.
Louisville, Ky.: Pentecostal Herald Press, 1899.
ISBN 0-8263-1748-0 (pbk.)
1. Andele, 1855–ca. 1935—Captivity, 1866.
2. Kiowa Indians—History.
3. Indian captivities—Texas.
I. Title.
E99.K5A536   1996
978.9′04′092—dc20
[B]
96-4424
CIP

Contents

CONTENTS

Introduction to
Andele:
The Mexican-Kiowa Captive

The end of the Civil War abolished chattel slavery in much of North America, but in the West another form of human bondage persisted. Under a regular column titled "Indian Matters," the October 20, 1866, issue of *The New Mexican* warned that the Probate Judge of San Miguel County had reported several recent depredations by Apaches in the vicinity of Las Vegas. Most alarming was a raid by a band of Mescaleros near the valley of San Gerónimo,

> where they killed a man...stole two children and a number of animals. They also killed three men, wounded three more and stole thirty or forty head of stock which they drove from the mountains beyond Upper Las Vegas.

Noting also that the Apaches had been so bold as to chase the stagecoach between Las Vegas and Fort Union, the columnist called for the punishment and confinement of these marauders, so they could "earn a living more honestly than by robbing our citizens." Forceful military action, and a program of civilization, would free New Mexico "from this incubus on our prosperity and peace of our territory."[1]

Whether from lack of interest or simple ignorance, the newspaper failed to report that the two captured children were José Andrés Martínez, age ten, and his younger nephew Pedro. Indian raids against peripheral villages in New Mexico were commonplace, and the seizure of women, children, and livestock the likely result. Pursuit and rescue might be attempted, but all too often proved fruitless. Most Anglos in Santa Fe probably agreed with Colonel E. V. Sumner's assessment some years earlier, when he claimed that

> this predatory warfare has been carried on for over 200 years, between the Mexican & the Indians, quite enough time to prove that unless some change is made the war will be interminable. They steal women and children, and cattle, from each other, and in fact carry on the war in all respects like two Indian nations.[2]

To American readers, the capture of the Martínez boys seemed all too much a part of a generally chaotic "savagery in the Territory. The only solution lay in a larger strategy of military conquest, forced reservation, and economic development that would put an end to this informal commerce, once and for all.

Today we are fortunate when we find evidence of the intimate human dimension beneath the patterns of raids and reprisals that characterized Indian-New Mexican relations: in this case, we have the life story of José Andrés Martínez himself. Captivity narratives provide insights into the lived experience of vulnerable and terrified individuals struggling to make sense of the unfamiliar and "exotic cultures in which they found themselves lodged. In the best of these narratives, we get rare first-hand accounts of American Indian societies—their daily rhythms, values, and the often heroic measures they employed to modify and preserve a severely threatened way of life. Finally, in particular cases we also catch glimpses of two societies engaged in the complicated process of intercultural negotiation; examining, rejecting, borrowing, and adopting elements of each other's lifeways.

Andele, The Mexican-Kiowa Captive provides such a narrative. Some thirty years after his capture while herding his father's cattle above San Gerónimo, José Andrés Martínez allowed the Methodist Minister J. J. Methvin to tell his story in print. Methvin hoped that the story, first published in 1899, would serve as a morality tale illustrating "the power of God unto salvation to everyone that believeth"(p.25). We cannot judge its merit in this regard, but for students of Plains Indian life in the nineteenth century it has proven a valuable resource, as did Andrés (Andele) himself to a generation of anthropologists studying Apache and Kiowa society. When read with Herman Lehmann's recently reprinted *Nine Years Among the Indians, 1870–1879*, a first-hand account of Lehmann's captivity with the Apaches and Comanches, we have two compelling portraits of Plains Indian societies at a crucial juncture in their histories.[3]

Without denying the reader the pleasure of discovery, Andele's experience may be briefly outlined. Seized by Chief Peso's band of Mescaleros in the autumn of 1866, Andrés witnessed the death of his nephew Pedro within a few days, then survived under the protection of a "little lame" Apache woman for several months. In late winter, a raiding band of Kiowas under Set-daya-ite (Heap-of-Bears or Many Bears) came upon the Apache encampment, and after a night of intense bartering, Andrés found himself exchanged for a mule, two buffalo robes, and a red blanket. Heap-of-Bears, using the services of Santiago, a Mexican captive who as an adult became a Kiowa warrior, assured Andrés that he purchased the boy as a replacement for his daughter Etonbo's recently deceased son. Renaming him Andele (or Andali, the exact phonetic transcription, for there is no R in the Kiowa-Tanoan language), Heap-of-Bears adopted the boy as his grandson, and returned with Andele to the main Kiowa encampment near the Wichita Mountains of Indian Territory (Oklahoma).

Andele adapted rapidly to the life of a Kiowa boy. Initiated into the *Pholiyoye* (Fulanyu or Rabbit) society, he learned to handle weapons and hunt with other boys of his age. Two years later, Heap-of-Bears died in an ill-omened raid against the Utes. In his first exposure to warfare, Andele witnessed the aftermath of George Armstrong Custer's slaughter of Black Kettle's Cheyenne band on the Washita.[4] At the age of sixteen, he joined the *Altoyuhe* (Herders) society, and accompanied his first raiding party into Texas, where he stole a mule and barely escaped the pursuit of some Texas Rangers.[5] Perhaps on the basis of this feat, the *Tsetanma* (Rulers of Horses) society invited him to join their order, within which he remained throughout his life. Andele's induction into these societies indicates how completely the Kiowas had accepted him as a kinsman.

Andele's adult years saw hard times for the Kiowas. Under President Ulysses S. Grant's Peace Policy (1869–82), they had been ordered to remain on a reservation with their Comanche allies in Indian Territory, with Fort Sill as headquarters for the Indian agent monitoring them. Assigned Lawrie Tatum, a Quaker missionary from Iowa, the Kiowas were expected to emulate his Christian example and become "civilized" farmers of wheat and corn. Colonel Benjamin H. Grierson, commanding the Tenth Cavalry and representing the military arm of the Peace Policy, was charged with protecting the Indians from white encroachments and interdicting renegade Indian raiders. Using rations of coffee, sugar, and corn, Tatum attempted to entice his Kiowa charges into a settled life, but corrupt supplymasters and drought kept the Indians on the verge of starvation. Heeding the call of tradition and necessity, Kiowa and Comanche warriors continued to make stock-and-captive raids into Texas and New Mexico. Tatum's payments of $100.00 apiece for repatriated captives proved the best source of revenue for the struggling tribes. Andele, however, refused Tatum's offer to purchase his freedom, preferring to remain with his Kiowa family.

In 1871, some Kiowas attacked the Warren wagon train in Jack County, Texas, killing seven teamsters and stealing forty-one mules. Grierson ordered the leaders arrested, and the Kiowas lost an important warrior when Satank (Set-an-gya or Sitting Bear) attempted to escape imprisonment and was killed by soldiers outside Ft. Sill. Satanta (Set-tain-te or White Bear) and Ado'eette (Big Tree) also suffered arrest and prosecution at this time. Satanta's sentence was commuted two years later, but he found himself imprisoned again after the Wichita Agency Uprising and Red River War of 1874–75. After General Nelson Miles suppressed this last-gasp resistance on the southern plains, he transported seventy-two Kiowa and Comanche warriors to Fort Marion in St. Augustine, Florida. Satanta remained in Texas, and took his own life in 1878, jumping from the second floor window of the State Penitentiary hospital.

With their military power extinguished, Andele and his Kiowa kinspeople sought to make the best of their new conditions. In the early 1880s, Andele approached Indian Agent George Hunt and requested training as a blacksmith in the Indian Agency shop. As memories of his family in New Mexico resurfaced, he asked Agency physician Hugh Tobin to write his brother Dionicio Martínez in Las Vegas, announcing Andele's interest in a reunion. After two years of anxious waiting, Dionicio responded, and Andele revisited the site of his capture. His aged mother received him warmly, but he left the family after only four years in New Mexico, feeling "his interests were all identified with the Kiowa, and he had learned to love them" (p. 120).

Upon his return to Indian Territory, Andele suffered a crisis of faith in "Indian medicine," converted to Methodism, and began teaching industrial arts in the Methvin Institute near Anadarko. Since his Kiowa wife Ti-i-ti (White Sage) had died during his absence, he courted and married the Methodist matron Emma McWhorter in 1893, with whom he adopted two orphan girls, one a Cherokee and another a Mexican-Kiowa mixed-blood. One year later, he began a new role as interpreter and spokesman for his people, travelling to Washington, D.C. with a Kiowa, Apache, and Comanche delegation to oppose allotment of reservation lands under the Dawes Act of 1887.[6] Until his death in the 1930s, he would continue to act as a mediator between Indian and white society.

ANDELE'S CAPTIVITY IN HISTORICAL AND CULTURAL PERSPECTIVE

Although a rare and valuable case of published reminiscence, Andele's captivity was but one of hundreds of such experiences in the southwest borderlands. Throughout the eighteenth and nineteenth centuries, Indians and Europeans engaged in a large-scale, multi-directional trade in human captives. Even as *The New Mexican* reported the capture of the two boys near San Gerónimo, the parish records of eastern New Mexican villages like Mora, Las Vegas, and San Miguel detailed the baptisms of dozens of *inditos criados* (Indian "servant children) obtained through capture or purchase on the plains. By the 1860s, more than 4,000 *indios gentiles* ("heathen Indians) resided in New Mexican households and villages, their status ranging from that of slaves to adopted kinspeople.[7] Likewise, conservative estimates of Euroamerican captives (and their descendants) resident in southern Plains tribes suggest they numbered between 10 and 20 percent of tribal populations.[8] Thus, for the Kiowas in 1870, captives and mixed-blood offspring may have numbered some 200 to 400 of the tribal census of 1,879 men, women and children.[9]

Certainly, Andele's narrative contains numerous references to Mexican and white captives among the Apaches and Kiowas. One of his Apache captors speaks of the "Mexican blood" in his own veins (p. 33), and Andele's purchase by Heap-of-Bears is arranged through the services of Santiago (pp. 45–48). Santiago may be the same man as Somtotleti, the Mexican captive who refuses to abandon Heap-of-Bears to fight the Utes alone, and dies by his side (pp. 67–68). Andele includes a whole chapter on Tahan, a white captive from Texas who escapes recapture and participates in the Battle of the Washita in 1868 (pp. 87–92).[10] We should note as well that Mokine, with whom Andele rides on his raiding initiation, was a "Black Mexican" captive taken in 1852, who later became protector of the sacred *Taimé* Sun Dance medicine bundle, and a Sun Dance assistant.[11]

Captive-taking seems to have served a complex web of purposes relating to prestige, population needs, and economic incentives. Andele's Apache captor claims his achievement would "make him a chief," perhaps meaning an elevation to respected warrior status. Heap-of-Bears' purchase of Andele, however, may have been more an act of an already prestigious man who simply wished to soothe his daughter's grief and add to his large extended household. Additional kinspeople meant additional labor as well; captive boys worked as herders, and captive women tanned buffalo hides for that increasingly lucrative trade.[12]

But it also appears that prestige and population considerations could be overruled by the sale or ransom value of captives. Partly due to Spanish New Mexico's demands for "slaves, Indian captives and ransomed New Mexicans had long brought two or three horses, blankets, and firearms in sales at semiannual *rescates*, "ransoms, or trade fairs. Until about 1800, Plains Apaches comprised the bulk of these *indios de rescate*; after that time, according to baptismal entries, Utes and Navajos dominated. The Kiowas and Comanches usually acted as suppliers, rather than victims, of this commerce in captives.[13]

Although the New Mexican aspect of this traffic lessened by the 1870s, the market continued in Texas, where in Jack County alone Kiowas and Comanches had seized more than 200 citizens between 1859 and 1871.[14] Recognizing that the Indians might require financial incentive to keep their victims alive, agent Lawrie Tatum continued customary "ransoms, once redeeming fourteen white and twelve Mexican captives from the Kiowa in a single purchase costing the agency $1,500. Andele claims that Texan residents Mrs. Koozer and her daughter were the last captives for whom agents paid ransom money (pp. 97–98).

White captives like the Koozers, Sarah Ann Horn, and Cynthia Ann Parker, famous mother of Quanah Parker, last Chief of the Quahada Comanches, have received the bulk of scholarly attention.[15] Andele's story is one of only three extant narratives of New Mexican captives known to this author, and by far the richest of the three.[16] Andele's story enlivens historical evidence that New Mexicans experienced the captive trade for a much longer duration, and in larger numbers, than ever did Anglo-Americans. With this in mind, we can look at the history of his Martínez family to understand some of the processes and pressures that culminated in his captivity.

THE VIEW FROM NEW MEXICO

Andele claims that his grandfather, Antonio José Martín, came to New Mexico from "Old Mexico" in 1773. The fact that immigration from Mexico did increase the *vecino* (citizen) population (which nearly tripled from 6,329 to 16,358 between 1765 and 1790) during the era of the Bourbon reforms lends general support to this statement.[17] Baptismal and census records seem to confirm his memory as well. Antonio José Martín appears in the Santa Fe census of 1790, and again in the military muster of 1800.[18] Antonio José must have married in the 1790s, for in the La Cienega census of 1821 he dwelt in a household with María Manuela Tafolla that included six children, the second of whom was Juan Pedro, Andele's father.[19] By 1841 Juan had married Maria Paubla Padilla, some twenty years his junior and a descendent of the La Cienega Bacas.[20]

Long-term pressures and one major political event combined to send Andele's parents on a migration to the foothills of eastern New Mexico. By the early years of the nineteenth century, farming land in the Río Grande valley grew so scarce that the expanding New Mexican population began to settle beyond the traditional boundaries of the province. To the south and west, *pastores* extended their sheep-raising into the Rio Puerco and the lands of the Navajo.[21] In the north, *pobladores* attempted to establish farming villages in the San Juan and San Luis valleys, traditional homelands of the Ute.[22] But the most significant expansion was eastward, to the foothills and grasslands beyond the Sangre de Cristo mountains.

Expansion eastward commenced in the 1790s, as *llaneros* (plainsmen) engaged in informal exchange with Plains Indians, and later with the formal commerce of the Santa Fe–St. Louis trade, established a series of villages along the Pecos and Mora rivers. San Miguel del Vado (1794), San Jose del Vado (1803), Mora (1818), and Anton Chico (1822) each served as provisioning points for *Comanchero* traders and commercial caravans.[23] But the major incentive for eastern expansion came with the American conquest of 1846–47, when

Stephen Watts Kearney led an American Army of occupation into the province. Since relations with Plains Indians deteriorated after the conquest and during the American Civil War, frontier outposts like Fort Union, Fort Sumner, and Fort Stanton became crucial centers for defense and economic development. Offering high demand for livestock forage and soldiers' food provisions, and hard cash with which to pay, these forts acted as "pull factors" to New Mexicans on the fringes of a fragile subsistence-and-exchange economy.[24]

Sometime in the 1850s, Juan and Paubla Martín responded to these push-and-pull forces, and migrated with their children to Montón de Alamos, on the Sapello River between Fort Union and Las Vegas. On October 25, 1855, Paubla bore their fourth son, whom they baptized José Andrés Martín in the village church five days later.[25] Although Andele claims that his family was "one of influence and power" in the county (p. 9), this seems not to have been the case. In the census of 1860, his father is enumerated as an illiterate "farm laborer" in Montón de Alamos, with the family assigned no real or personal property of value.[26] Perhaps in an ill-fated attempt to escape Indian depredations along the Santa Fe Trail, the family moved twenty miles southwest in the 1860s, to the village of San Gerónimo, nestled in the foothill valley of Tecolote Creek. Just three weeks shy of his eleventh birthday, Andrés and Pedro drove Juan's few cattle to graze on the Medina meadows, where the Mescaleros seized them (pp. 30–33).

We know little more about Andele's family. His statement that Juan died with a "broken heart" after "three years of anxious search" finds support in the census of 1870, where the census-taker notes that Juan P. Martínez died of "consumption (tuberculosis) in May of that year. Andele's mother, Paubla, continued to "keep house in San Gerónimo, supported by her eldest son, Dionicio, and sixteen-year-old Regordio, both "farm laborers. Mercelina, her fourteen-year-old daughter, lived at home as well. The fear of Indian attack had not faded, for the census also noted that Miguel Jaramillo was "killed by Indians in July of 1869, on the trail between San Gerónimo and Las Vegas.[27]

Paubla would not see Andrés, her "muchochito, for another fifteen years, and when she did, his transformation into a mature Kiowa man, resplendent in his "Indian paraphernalia, must have made the reunion bittersweet. Perhaps she could see that his "interests were all identified with the Kiowa." Andele's return to his Indian kinspeople requires that we turn now to an examination of these, the people he had "learned to love."

THE KIOWAS' WORLD

The *Ga-i-gwu*, or "people with one-half (hair or face-paint) different" remain an enigma among Plains Indians.[28] Unlike their Comanche allies or Dakota enemies, Kiowa origins have proved difficult to trace along archaeological or linguistic paths. Their language derives from the Tanoan family, and bears closest affinity with the Tiwa sub-family spoken by the people of Taos, Sandia, and Isleta pueblos of New Mexico. Tribal origin narratives vaguely recall a migration across the Saskatchewan plains, and more specifically campsites and hunting areas in the Yellowstone region, where they made acquaintance with their long-time friends, the Crows.[29] According to European reckoning, Kiowas lived in the northern plains in the seventeenth century; however, the historical linguistic work of Nancy Hickerson may deepen their presence on the grasslands, and connect them to the "protohistoric" Jumanos of the southern plains.[30]

The Kiowas were well known to Spanish authorities in eighteenth-century New Mexico. By 1800, at least thirty-five Kiowas had received baptism in village churches, no doubt as *indios de rescate* purchased from other Plains groups at trade fairs.[31] In the same year, they conducted their first raids on the province, taking stock and captives in the Abiquiu area.[32] Significant for the story at hand, Kiowa historians recall that their forebears and the Comanches negotiated a lasting alliance at about this time, using the *rancho* (dwelling) and mediating services of a New Mexican *llanero* "friendly to both sides."[33] In 1807, the Kiowas celebrated a peace treaty with the Spanish at the Governor's Palace in Santa Fe, and received presents of blankets, tobacco, mirrors, and tools.[34]

Indeed, these agreements ushered in several decades of productive exchanges among the Kiowas, Comanches, and New Mexican *comancheros* and *ciboleros* (traders and buffalo hunters). The Kiowas and Comanches now raided Apache, Ute, and Navajo enemies for captives to sell at *rescates*, although they did, on occasion, plunder New Mexican villages and traders as well.[35]

The American conquest and Civil War destabilized the long-term informal economy of the Southern Plains. Troop movements, commercial caravans, and indiscriminate buffalo hunting all impinged upon Kiowa and Comanche autonomy, as did American attempts to restrict their territorial range. Between 1865 and 1875, the United States would wage an all-out campaign to "settle and civilize" the equestrians of the *Comanchería*.[36] Thus, Andele entered Kiowa society in the decade when their power waxed, then rapidly waned.

Andele's narrative serves as a rich source for descriptions of Kiowa culture during this epochal period. He gives first-hand accounts of captive adoption ritual among the Mescaleros and Kiowas, depicting both the terrifying and tender aspects of the experience. He describes seasonal hunting and trading patterns, warrior societies, and offers detailed observations on items of material culture like the *Pa-lo-tle-ton* buffalo robe bed (pp. 53–54). His description of the annual Sun Dance, in which a captive "Mexican" woman plays an honored role, has served as the starting point for anthropological investigation of this Plains-wide sacred event.[37] So too for the Scalp Dance, a three-week celebration in which we see the prominence of honor and revenge in Plains Indian warfare (pp. 61–64). Andele's own vision quest is carefully recounted, as is the dream in which he sees the war-shield he must obtain to secure his power (pp. 77–82).

The fact that Andele strove for status under the guidance of a "medicine man" suggests that he experienced remarkable good fortune in his adoption by Heap-of-Bears. Most captives in the Kiowas' ranked society fared not so well. Four hierarchical categories constituted Kiowa social organization: *óndei*, or successful warriors of noble bearing and generosity; *óndeigupa*, second to *óndei*, or people with noble qualities but without major military honors; *Koen*, or commoners without economic independence or military accomplishments; and *Dapóm*, or people without property, accomplishment, or even honor. Most captives who did not experience fortuitous adoption found themselves in this last rank, forced to attach themselves to wealthy families as dependent horse herders, butchers, and "chore wives." Although these ranks were to some degree hereditary, both commoners and "slaves" could move upward with honorable ser-

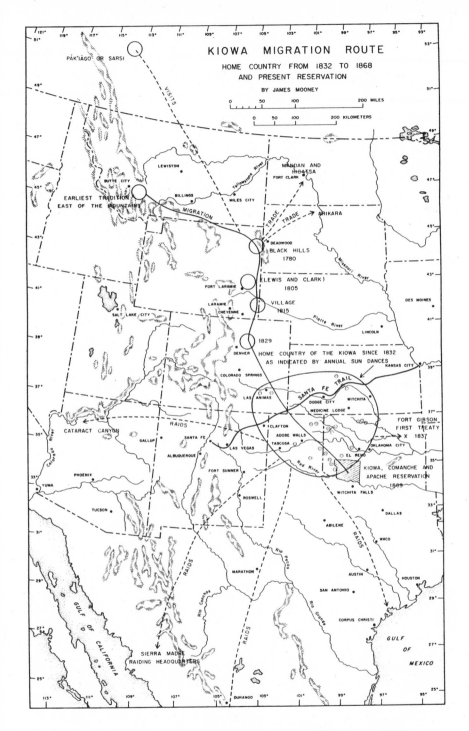

Kiowa Migrations and Home Territory, 1832–1868. Mooney 1898,
Smithsonian Institution.

vice to their patrons, achievements in warfare, or a marriage that gave them influential kin who could "raise them up" by bestowing "good names" and gifts of horses and other prestigious items.[38] In Andele's case, his family's wealth allowed him to offer blankets and other property in return for spiritual guidance, and equipped him with a horse and weapons for his first raid into Texas (pp. 82–86).

Andele also offers some important insights into gender and marriage in Kiowa society. Kiowa women make important contributions to their society's economy, especially as hide processors (in fact, Honzip-fa, his adoptive grandmother's name, means "tanner of hides").[39] Kiowa women both take advantage of and suffer within the "bridewealth" and easy divorce system of their culture: women are able to increase their status by absconding with higher status men, but may suffer beatings, mutilation, and even death if their former husband can summon sufficient family and social support for his action.[40] Andele himself participates in the full range of Kiowa marriage practices, "purchasing" his first wife, Tonko, for "one good pony and two buffalo robes." He suffers, however, when she elopes with a higher-status warrior. After Andele kills three of his rival's best horses, we see social approval of his action, and community-wide settlement of his complaint. Marrying again, he soon "puts away" his second wife because he finds her too old. Finally, he attains happiness with Ti-i-ti (White Sage), who tragically dies while Andele resides with his family in New Mexico from 1885 to 1889 (pp. 119–22).

Andele's experience serves as an example of the painful personal and spiritual adjustments that Indian people found themselves forced to make during the reservation period. Andele had taken quickly to Kiowa spiritual practice, which involved the ritualized "purchase" of "medicine" powers from elders of the óndei rank by aspiring younger men. At first glance we might suppose this a simple economic transaction, but exchanges of material goods cloaked profound spiritual meaning. A young man like Andele could not "decide" to purchase an elder's powers, he must first receive a potent dream or vision that justified his right to become a practitioner of such spiritual force.[41] Hence we see Andele "crying and worshipping" the medicine bundle of Sankadotie, the medicine chief. Still lacking a vision, he sponsors a "sweat house" ceremony, and finally receives the earnestly sought dream after fasting in the mountains. Yet even then, Sankadotie withholds the treasured shield, insisting that such power would become too "great a burden" to the young man. Finally, he dismisses Andele's pleadings, saying "you have not paid me enough yet;" in essence, 'you have not yet the power for such medicine (pp. 77–82).

Although Andele earns some medicines, and even practices a few healing rites, military defeat and the reservation system cut the underpinnings from beneath traditional spiritual and social life. With customary avenues to power and prestige closed to him, Andele suffers a crisis of identity, and experiments with repatriation as a New Mexican. Finding his heart still drawn to his Indian kinspeople, he begins to seek accommodation with the Methodist missionaries among the Kiowa. If we are to trust Reverend Methvin's account alone, Andele's conversion seems decisive and complete. Yet other sources suggest this may have been a painful balancing of Indian and white spiritual traditions. In 1923, according to Kiowa historians, Andele participated in a Native American Church peyote ritual, and closed the all-night ceremony with a prayer from the Bible he carried with him into the sweat lodge.[42]

Even in his marriage to the Methodist matron Emma McWhorter, we see suggestions of a cultural balancing act. With no children of their own, the couple adopt two Indian girls, a poignant reenactment of Andele's own experience with fictive kinship. His role as interpreter and delegate in the Kiowa protest against the Allotment Act reveals him as deeply committed to at least some customary principles, and his willingness to serve as an anthropological informant attests to his continuing pride in Kiowa history and culture. In this regard, he seems similar to Black Elk, Andele's more famous counterpart among the Oglala Sioux, who, although he embraced Catholicism later in life, still hoped to guide his people toward completion of the Sacred Hoop of Life.[43]

ANDELE'S NARRATIVE AS A LITERARY TEXT

One last aspect of Andele's story deserves some discussion: its position within the tradition of Christian missionary tracts and captivity narratives in general. Readers will note the heavy-handed moralizing judgments that the Reverend J. J. Methvin injects regularly into Andele's tale. Offensive as they seem to us today, they serve to remind us that most of the captivity narratives with which scholars work were the product of evangelical Protestants bent on the cultural destruction and moral regeneration of people they deemed degenerate, degraded, and uncivilized.

The Federal Peace Policy (1869–82) initiated under President Grant effectively placed Indian reservations under church control, with the intent that Christian guidance would work a cultural transformation more efficiently than military suppression. In practice, the U.S. Army became the hammer of the civilizing mission, reducing and congregating militant Indians around agencies where the "gentle tamers" could work their miracles. While Orthodox and Hicksite Quakers initiated many such missions, they were soon joined by Catholic, Methodist, Presbyterian, Baptist, and Episcopal evangelists eager to work in the "Fields of the Lord."[44]

Lawrie Tatum and his Quaker associates took up the first missionary activities among the Kiowa and Comanche, but soon found that their pacifist approach struck few chords with their martially oriented wards. The Episcopalians under the Reverend J. B. Wicks made the next attempt in 1883, building a church at the new Agency in Anadarko.[45] They too abandoned the field, but in 1887 Methodist Bishop Galloway and his subordinate, the Reverend Methvin, established a parsonage, church, and Indian school near the agency headquarters. Two years later, according to Methvin, Andele cautiously approached the Bishop and began his conversion to Christianity, and became a teacher at the Indian school (pp. 119–22).

Methvin took his work seriously. Targeting Indian spiritual practices and polygamous marriage as the root of their barbarism, he engaged in a life-long struggle with Quanah Parker to suppress peyote worship in Parker's Native American Church, and to force the Quahada chief to divest himself of two of his three wives.[46] With Andele's assistance, he brought Kiowa and Comanche children into the Methvin Institute, where in a symbolic initiation to "kill the Indian and save the Man," their long hair was shorn and their Indian clothing exchanged for shirts and trousers. Grieving parents were told to "return home and not come back until the children had adjusted to school life."[47]

Methvin clearly intended Andele's narrative to serve as an example that "a people. . .in whom there was so little upon which to base a hope of building a civilization" could be brought to salvation through God's works (p. 25). Indeed, he found Andele's story compelling evidence of God's "mysterious ways," for "in the apparent calamity that had come to Andrés in his capture, God was overruling it all in preparing him for a life that would glorify him" (p. 120). Perhaps the most remarkable element of Andele's text is that the intelligence, humor, affection, and honor of the Kiowa people survive Methvin's condescending and moralizing interjections.

In its effort to show "a sense of God's pardoning love and redeeming grace," Andele's narrative seems closer in some respects to Puritan captivity narratives of the seventeenth century (like that of Mary Rowlandson [1682]) than many of its nineteenth century contemporaries. That Methvin acted as an amanuensis (taking and rearranging Andele's dictation), fits this tradition. Like Puritan narratives, it contains elements of spiritual autobiography, sermonizing, jeremiad, and the secular adventure story, but combines these with the ethnoexoticism of later captivity stories.[48]

Andele himself knew that Methvin's narrative contained errors (the mislabelling of the *Qoitsenko* society as "Dog Soldiers," instead of "Sacred Dogs" [horses]), which he explained to Robert Lowie in 1915 were "due to his inadequate knowledge of English at the time of its composition."[49] We cannot know how thoroughly he subscribed to Methvin's interpretation of his conversion experience, but he does seem to have retained a greater respect for Indian spiritual practices than Methvin would have it. His participation in peyote ceremonies seems not an evangelizing effort, but rather an attempt to find a place for himself in a religion that was itself a synthesis of Indian and Christian belief.[50] Rather than dismiss Methvin's role in Andele's narrative as overbearing and arrogant, we should treat it as a subtext to the larger narrative, with its own historical merit.

Captivity experiences continue to fascinate popular audiences as well as scholars. Successful films like *Little Big Man* (1970), *The Emerald Forest* (1985), *Dances with Wolves* (1990), and *Black Robe* (1991) owe some of their appeal to prominent captivity themes. Scholars increasingly see captivity tales as avenues to investigate cultural values and practices in non-Indian and native societies alike. John Demos has recently offered *The Unredeemed Captive: A Fam-*

ily Story from Early America, in which the captivity of Eunice Williams (1704–86) serves to illuminate Mohawk, French Canadian, and Puritan New England societies.[51] June Namias's *White Captives: Gender and Ethnicity on the American Frontier* looks at women's narratives across time and space to examine changing notions of gender, ethnicity, and sexuality.[52] *Andele, The Mexican-Kiowa Captive* remains an important member of this literary family, and a key document in the history of our own multi-ethnic Southwest borderlands.

NOTES

1. *The New Mexican,* October 20, 1866, p. 2; microfilm in the New Mexico State Records Center, Santa Fe.

2. Colonel E.V. Sumner to General John G. Jones, Fort Conrad, New Mexico, November 20, 1851, in Annie H. Abel, ed. *The Official Correspondence of James S. Calhoun, while Indian Agent at Santa Fe and Superintendent of Indian Affairs in New Mexico* (Washington, D.C. 1915) p. 445.

3. Herman Lehmann, *Nine Years Among the Indians, 1870–1879* J. Martin Hunter, ed. (Albuquerque, 1993[1927]); for an overview of Southern Plains Indian history in the nineteenth century, see Rupert N. Richardson, *The Comanche Barrier to South Plains Settlement* (Glendale, 1933); for a recent narrative history, see Stanley Noyes, *Los Comanches: The Horse People, 1751–1845* (Albuquerque, 1993).

4. Methvin incorrectly dates this event as occurring in 1870 (p. 87), when it actually took place on November 27, 1868. In a surprise attack on Black Kettle's peaceful camp, Custer's 7th Cavalry killed 103 men, women and children, and destroyed nearly 1,000 horses. See Maurice Boyd, *Kiowa Voices: Myths, Legends, and Folktales* (Fort Worth, 1983) pp. 172–82 for the Kiowa role in covering the Cheyenne retreat.

5. For Andele's induction into Kiowa Men's Societies, see Robert H. Lowie's "Societies of the Kiowa," *Anthropological Papers of the American Museum of Natural History* v. 11 (Washington, D.C. 1916) pp. 839–81. Andele served as Lowie's principle informant during his fieldwork of June, 1915.

6. See James Mooney, "Calendar History of the Kiowa Indians," *Seventeenth Annual Report of the Bureau of American Ethnology,* Part II. (Washington, D.C. 1979[1898]) pp. 224–25.

7. The best enumeration of Indian captives in New Mexican society may be found in David M. Brugge, *Navajos in the Catholic Church Records of*

New Mexico, 1694–1875 (Tsaile, 1985).

8. In 1830, Jean Luis Berlandier counted 500–600 "creole" captives among the Comanche population of 10–12,000; since most of these women and children would remain with their captors, and form families there, a second-generation captive and mixed-blood population of 1,500 seems reasonable. See John C. Ewers, ed., *The Indians of Texas in 1830*, by Jean Luis Berlandier (Washington, D.C. 1969[1844]) pp. 76, 83, 114, 119. James Mooney, in his "Calendar History of the Kiowa Indians" estimates that "at least one-fourth of the whole number have more or less of captive blood" (pp. 235–36). If we treat Jane Richardson's 1940 case study of Kiowa law as a cross section of society in the late 19th century, her 92 cases feature 183 protagonists of whom 23 are captives or of mixed descent, or 12.5% of the population. See Jane Richardson, "Law and Status Among the Kiowa Indians," *Monographs of the American Ethnological Society* Vol. 1 (New York, 1940); The 1933 Ethnographic Field School out of Santa Fe estimated that mixed-bloods, primarily of Mexican descent, comprised as much as 70% of Comanche society; see E. Adamson Hoebel, "The Political Organization and Law Ways of the Comanche Indians," *Memoirs of the American Anthropological Association*, no. 54 (Menasha, Wisconsin, 1940).

9. *Annual Report of the Secretary of the Interior, 1870*. (Washington, D.C., 1870) p. 728.

10. For Tehan's narrative of the Washita fight, see Maurice Boyd, *Kiowa Voices: Myths, Legends and Folktales* Vol. II (Forth Worth, 1983) pp. 172–82. This entry also calls into question Andele's account of Tehan's death at Napawat's hands, for Tehan told his story to Susan Peters sometime after 1917.

11. The *Taimé* came to the Kiowas in 1765, when an Arapaho man, who had obtained the sacred figure from the Crows, married a Kiowa woman. See Maurice Boyd, *Kiowa Voices*, 47–59; 159–61; Mokine also married Satanta's widow Zoam-tay ("Born-with-her-Teeth"), evidence of his high status among the Kiowa. For a legal case in 1888 that reveals his powers as a sorcerer, see Jane Richardson, "Law and Status Among the Kiowa Indians" (New York, 1940) pp. 54–55.

12. Both Sarah Ann Horn (1837) and Rosita Rodriguez (1846) wrote that they were set to work to tan hides almost immediately. See "A Narrative of the Captivity of Sarah Ann Horn and Her Two Children," reprinted in Carl Coke Rister, *Comanche Bondage* (Lincoln, 1989 [1955]); "Rosita Rodrigues to Don Miguel Rodrigues, January 13, 1846," in the Bexar Archives, Barker

History Center, University of Texas, Austin.

13. For a dated and poorly referenced treatment of this commerce, see L.R. Bailey, *Indian Slave Trade in the Southwest* (Los Angeles, 1966); for a current analysis, see James F. Brooks, "Captives and Cousins: Violence, Kinship and Community in the New Mexico Borderlands, 1680–1880." (Unpublished Ph.D dissertation, University of California, Davis, 1995).

14. Lee Cutler, "Lawrie Tatum and the Kiowa Agency, 1869–1873," *Arizona and the West* (Autumn, 1971) pp. 221–44, citing Governor E.J. Davis to President Ulysses S. Grant, March 22, 1871, Letters Received, Office of Indian Affairs, Roll 377.

15. For Cynthia Ann Parker's story, see Margaret Schmidt Hacker, *Cynthia Ann Parker* (El Paso, 1990); for a narrative history drawn from captive experiences, see Carl Coke Rister, *Border Captives: The Traffic in Prisoners by Southern Plains Indians, 1835–1875* (Norman, 1940).

16. Rosita Rodrigues' narrative (see note 12) is simply a two-page letter to her father, but does contain some important details about captives' work, and the fact that her little boy remained with his Indian captors, apparently quite happily; a manuscript titled "La Cautiva" in the Kit Carson Archives of Taos, New Mexico, tells the story of the captivity of Refugio Gurriola, seized in Sonora in 1858 by Yaquis and later sold to the Apaches. She escaped in 1864 to Tierra Amarilla, New Mexico, and later became a resident of Taos, where she married Teófilo Martínez, a soldier.

17. See Donald C. Cutter, "An Anonymous Statistical Report on New Mexico in 1765," *New Mexico Historical Review* Vol. 50, No. 4 (1975) pp. 347–52; Alicia V. Tjarks, "Demographic, Ethnic, and Occupational Structure of New Mexico, 1790," *The Americas* (Vol. 35, No. 1 (1978) pp. 45–88; for an in-depth treatment of demographic and economic change in New Mexico during this period, see Ross H. Frank, "From Settler to Citizen: Economic Development and Cultural Change in Late Colonial New Mexico, 1750–1820" (Unpublished Ph.D. dissertation, University of California, Berkeley, 1992).

18. Census of 1790, *villa* of Santa Fe, p. 428 (Elizabeth Olmstead, comp., p. 71); and the Military Muster of Santa Fe, November 6, 1800; both in the New Mexico State Records Center, Santa Fe.

19. La Cienega census of 1821, Household #28, in the Durango Archives, Chihuahua, Mexico. This census notes Juan's age as 22.

20. Santa Fe Baptisms, Archdiocesan Archives of Santa Fe, January 20, 1819, for Paubla's baptismal information.

21. See John O. Baxter, *Las Carneradas: Sheep Trade in New Mexico, 1700–1860* (Albuquerque, 1987).

22. For this expansion, see Francis Swadesh Quintana, *Pobladores: Hispanic Americans of the Ute Frontier* (Aztec, 1991 [1974]).

23. Charles L. Kenner, *The Comanchero Frontier* (Norman, 1994[1969]); also Frances Levine, "Economic Perspectives on the Comanchero Trade," in Katherine A. Spielmann, ed., *Farmers, Hunters, and Colonists: Interaction between the Southwest and the Southern Plains* (Tucson, 1991) pp. 155–70.

24. See Darlis Miller, *Soldiers and Settlers: Military Supply in the Southwest, 1861–1885* (Albuquerque, 1989).

25. Las Vegas Baptismal Book, Montón de Alamos, p. 124, in the New Mexico State Records Center, Santa Fe.

26. New Mexico Territorial Census of 1860, village of Montón de Alamos, San Miguel County, p. 312.

27. Territorial Census of 1870, village of San Gerónimo, San Miguel County, Household #47 p. 5 (Frame 442); and Schedule Two, "Persons who died during the Year," New Mexico State Records Center, Santa Fe.

28. James Mooney suggests that this name derives from a customary hair-style in which Kiowa warriors cut the right side of their hair short, above the ear, to display ear pendants, and let the left side grow long, braided and wrapped in otter skin. It may have earlier roots in a distinctive tattooing, if indeed the Kiowa descend from the Jumanos, who were known for their facial tattoos. Mooney, "Calendar History," p. 150.

29. Maurice Boyd, *Kiowa Voices*, pp. 1–12.

30. Nancy P. Hickerson, "Ethnogenesis in the Great Plains: Jumano to Kiowa?" Paper read at the annual meeting of the American Association for the Advancement of Science, Chicago, Ill, 1991; "Kiowa: The Resurgence of Tanoan in the Southern Plains," paper read at the annual meeting of the American Anthropological Association, San Francisco, CA, 1992; *The Jumanos: Hunters and Traders of the South Plains* (Austin, 1994).

31. David M. Brugge, "Some Plains Indians in the Church Records of New Mexico," *Plains Anthropologist* 10 (No. 29, 1965) pp. 181–89.

32. Pedro de Nava to Governor Fernando Chacón, October 7, 1800 [Twitchell #1511]; Chacón, summary of events between October 1 and 25, dated November 24, 1800 [Twitchell #1517], *The Spanish Archives of New Mexico* Vol. II, Ralph Emerson Twitchell, ed. (Glendale, 1914).

33. Mooney, *Calendar History of the Kiowa*, pp. 162–63; see also Eliza-

beth E.F. John, "An Earlier Chapter of Kiowa History," *New Mexico Historical Review* Vol. 60, No. 4 (1985) pp. 379–96. John puts the date in the later half of 1806.

34. John, "An Earlier Chapter," pp. 389–91.

35. Forrest D. Monahan, Jr., "The Kiowas and New Mexico, 1800–1845, *Journal of the West* Vol. 8, No. 1 (January, 1969) pp. 67–75.

36. Charles L. Kenner, *The Comanchero Frontier*, p. 115ff.

37. See, for example, Ralph Linton, "The Comanche Sun Dance," *American Anthropologist* n.s. 37 (1935) pp. 420–28. Alice Marriott, in *The Ten Grandmothers* (Norman, 1945) pp. 53–56 complicates the role of the captive woman in procuring the sacred Sun Dance tree, noting that "she had to be a captive, because what she was going to do was [spiritually] dangerous, and you could not risk one of your own women to do it; she had to be dressed beautifully because what she was to do was a great honor, even if she died doing it."

38. I have here simplified the categories and orthographies of Kiowa ranks, drawing upon the most thorough treatment of rank and social status among the Kiowas in Bernard Mishkin, *Rank and Warfare Among the Plains Indians* (Lincoln, 1992[1940]) esp. pp. 35–56, with a new introduction by Morris W. Foster. Mishkin's informants counted Heap-of-Bears (#9, therein called "Tseitáinte") among the twenty-five most important men of the tribe circa 1870, and one of twelve tribal headmen (p. 54).

39. M. Boyd, p. 157. Hon-zip-fa was also the adoptive mother of Guo-la-te, a three-year-old New Mexican boy taken in 1854, suggesting that Heap-of-Bears used captivity to augment his family throughout his life. See M. Boyd, *Kiowa Voices*, pp. 155–58.

40. Jane Collier's *Marriage and Inequality in Classless Societies* (Stanford, 1988) discusses marriage systems of the Comanche, Kiowa, and Cheyenne in comparative perspective.

41. For a description of the generational transmission of spiritual powers, see Alice Marriott's chapter, "Hunting for Power," in *The Ten Grandmothers*, pp. 41–49.

42. M. Boyd, "A Peyote Meeting: 1923" in *Kiowa Voices* pp. 278–83.

43. See Raymond J. DeMaillie, ed., *The Sixth Grandfather: Black Elk's Teachings Given to John G. Neihardt* (Lincoln, 1984); for a treatment of Black Elk from the standpoint of literary criticism, see Julian Rice, *Black Elk's Story: Distinguishing its Lakota Purpose* (Albuquerque, 1991).

44. The best treatment of this policy is found in Robert H. Keller, Jr.,

American Protestantism and United States Indian Policy, 1869–1882 (Lincoln, 1983).

45. Mooney, "Calendar History," p. 219.

46. William T. Hagan, *Quanah Parker, Comanche Chief* (Norman, 1993) pp. 52, 72, 76, 89, 91.

47. M. Boyd, "Calendar History," pp. 290–92.

48. For the Puritan tradition, see Alden T. Vaughan and Edward W. Clark, "Cups of Common Calamity: Puritan Captivity Narratives as Literature and History," in Vaughan and Clark, eds., *Puritan Among the Indians: Accounts of Captivity and Redemption, 1676–1724* (Cambridge, 1981) pp. 1–28; for attitudes in the 19th century, see Roy Harvey Pearce, *The Savages of America: A Study of the Indian and the Idea of Civilization* (Baltimore, 1965); for narratives themselves, see Charles Coke Rister, *Border Captives: The Traffic in Prisoners by Southern Plains Indians, 1835–1875* (Norman, 1940).

49. Lowie, "Societies of the Kiowa," p. 839.

50. See Omar C. Stewart, *Peyote Religion* (Norman, 1987) for a thorough treatment of the Native American Church.

51. John Demos, *The Unredeemed Captive: A Family Story from Early America* (New York, 1994).

52. June Namias, *White Captives: Gender and Ethnicity on the American Frontier* (Chapel Hill, 1993).

Foreword

It has been more than a quarter of a century since "Andele, or the Kiowa-Mexican Captive" was first off the press. It has run through several editions, but there seems to be a demand for its continued publication.

So we issue this edition, with a supplement to tell of some things omitted in previous chapters, and to give some of the many things of interest that have transpired in the life of Andele in more recent years.

From the time of his capture down to the present, his life is one of thrilling interest and historic value, for in no other volume can so much reliable information concerning Indian life and habits, which are already almost a thing of the past, be found in so short a space and in so pleasing form.

We send forth, therefore, this new edition with the added supplement with confident expectation that the reader will find its perusal both pleasant and profitable.

J.J.M.

Preface

This is a volume of simple narrative without any effort at literary skill. It is not fiction, but truth; and truth is stranger than fiction. In connection with this story of the life of "Andele" among the Kiowas, much of the habits, customs, and superstitions of the Indians is given: and, indeed, no incident is related that does not set forth some phase of Indian life in its real light. When historical events are given there may be some discrepancy as to exact dates, but the actual events themselves are as related. The condition of things, as exhibited in this little volume, is fast passing away; indeed, many changes have already taken place, and the Indians are taking on gradually, but surely, a real and permanent civilization. Years of association with the Indian has increased my hopefulness for him. His salvation and his development into a permanent and substantial civilization are as bright as the promises of God. This is being demonstrated all the while, as the work of the church and the government goes on with them.

To start with, there never was a people, perhaps in whom there was so little upon which to base a hope of building a civilization. No homes or home life, no enterprise, no written language; but wild, nomadic, barbarous, savage, their glory the glory of war and plunder, their religion that of bloody revenge, the conscience and moral instinct dead. But among the wild tribes, as well as the civilized, the gospel proves the power of God unto salvation to every one that believeth. There is a wonderful chapter to be written in this respect, but what God has wrought among them will be told in a separate volume later on.

The author sends forth this true story of Andele's life with the hope that the young people of the church to whom it is affectionately dedicated may find both pleasure and profit in reading it.

J.J.M.

Index to
Supplement

ANDELE
THE MEXICAN-KIOWA
CAPTIVE

I

The Martínez Family.

Juan Martínez was born in June, 1807. He was of pure Castilian blood. In 1773 his father, when yet quite a boy, had come with his parents from Old Mexico and settled in the United States, near Las Vegas, in New Mexico. At the age of thirty-four he fell in love with a beautiful young lady, a Bastago, herself also of pure Castilian blood, Senorita Paulita Padillo, and married her in 1841. It was a happy union, and, from the first, prosperity smiled upon them.

They settled soon after at Los Alamos, but after a few years removed to near San Gerónimo, twelve miles west of Las Vegas, a place lying between Gerónimo and Hot Springs, in a vicinity where, as yet, no one else had settled. Here were born to them four sons: Victorino, Dionicio, Regordio, and Andrés, and three daughters, Francisca, Sabina, and Marcilina. With this interesting household of seven children the Martínez family became one of influence and power as population increased and the country developed.

Andrés was the youngest son, and perhaps, physically, the weakest in the household, but of quick wit and acute mental perception. Living on the frontier, exposed to the frequent marauding, plundering expeditions of the various tribes of wild Indians wandering over the country, they grew up inured to dangers and equipped for emergencies. People by necessity become quick witted and skilled in the midst of the trying emergencies that come up in a frontier life. Many a latent power and sleeping faculty have been stirred to life and called into action in the face of great danger or extreme emergency, that, in luxury and ease, would have slept on forever undeveloped. Trials, conflicts, emergencies, are necessary to arouse and develop the latent faculties of our being, hence we should count it all joy when they come.

Often had the Martínez family to guard themselves against the stealthy attacks of the wild Mescaleros and other marauding tribes, and at the time this history beings (1866), there were rumors that the Apaches were prowling about in the vicinity, but as such rumors had been constantly circulated during the past month, the community had grown careless and no watch kept up. Evil be the day when a man ceases to watch.

II

The Mescaleros Capture Andrés.

It was a bright, beautiful morning, October 6, 1866. The Martínez family were astir early, for wheat threshing was on hand for the day, and everyone who could be of service must be called into requisition.

"Andrés," called Juan Martínez, "my little boy, you must herd the cows to-day, for I shall need Regordio to aid in the wheat threshing. Drive the cows out to the range and keep good watch over them, and about noon I will come to you and bring you some dinner. Be a good boy. *Adios.*" Just at this moment little Pedro, Sabina's son, set up a plea to go with Andrés, but, being refused, he watched his opportunity, ran away, and joined him on the way.

Poor little fellow! He little dreamed what this act of disobedience would bring him. He little thought that he was turning his back on his home forever; that the music of mother's voice and the light of her loving smiles would never more gladden his little heart; that his own life would be put out as a candle by cruel hands, and his own little body, pierced and bleeding, would be left out on the broad prairie along among the sage weeds and grass to feed the coyotes and the wolves.

'Tis so often thus, in the prospect of present enjoyment, the happy youth loses sight of disobedience's dire results, till destruction comes and despair like night settles down forever.

"We will drive the cows into yonder little *vega*, Pedro," said Andrés, "for there the grazing is good, there is no timber to hide them, and we can watch them better as we play there in the edge of the timber."

"All right," said Pedro, and they turned the cows in that direction. Soon the herd was comfortably grazing with heads toward the southwest, and the boys, as they watched, were playing in a cluster of low oaks at the edge of the valley.

The morning fast passed. One hour had gone and then another. "Look," said Andrés, "the cows seem to be uneasy and are heading for home. Let us run around them and turn them back." With some difficulty having accomplished this, they resumed their play in the oak thicket, gathering together and arranging in groups to represent herds, the white stones that lay scattered here and there upon the ground, and naming individual stones for the familiar old milk cows in the herd they were watching. Suddenly the sound of voices arrested their attention.

"Father is coming," said Andrés, "for he said he would come out about noon to see me and bring me some dinner. It is rather early, but I am getting hungry anyhow, and"—but looking up, the little boys were filled with dismay to discover, about fifty paces away, coming directly toward them, a band of wild Mescalero Apaches, with painted faces, and shields, and bows and arrows. Some of them were riding burros belonging to Andrés' father, which they had doubtless stolen from the farm the night before.

But their attention, before discovering the boys, who had now crouched down amid the bushes, was directed to a Mexican man, who was traveling the road which passed through the edge of the little valley towards San Gerónimo. The Mexican had two burros, loaded with flour, which he was driving along before him.

"Lie down, Pedro," said Andrés, "keep still, they see the Mexican yonder and are started in pursuit, and when they are fully passed, if they do not discover us, we will run for yonder timber and make our escape for home. Keep still, Pedro," continued Andrés, "keep still, your life depends upon it. If you make a noise, they will find us out and we are lost. It may be they will not see us. Keep still."

As the savage band passed on, their interest fully set on the Mexican, and the boys were just in the act of slipping down through the low bushes that lined the valley to the timber beyond, they were discovered by two Apaches, who, for some reason, had wandered from the main band, and who now ran upon the boys with a wild shout of delight. Rejoicing at the prospect of being chiefs, each singled out his boy, ran upon him, struck him with his spear and then claimed him as a captive. This is a custom among the Indians, that whosoever first strikes a captive, or kills and scalps an enemy, becomes a hero, and great honor is done him on his return home, and he is ever after considered a great chief. His word commands attention, his wishes must be respected. It matters not whether he kills a man or captures a babe, he secures a title to chiefhood.

It may be stated here that it is not often that Indians kill little children, if they can carry them off, and it is a marvelous fact that, notwithstanding their fearful savage natures, they often show the tenderest affection for children. But it seems that the Mescaleros are among the most abandoned and cruel, and the two who had captured the boys hurried them along, calling out in mock tenderness, "Come on, come on, little boys, we will take you to see your mother, you must go to see your mother, she is crying for you now," until they reached the band who had gathered around the Mexican and his burros. They had cut the flour sacks open and scattered the flour to the prairie winds, and stripped the Mexican of every rag of clothing, till he stood there naked and trembling, his yellow skin glistening in the sunlight of that October morning, a pitiable sight.

The two boys and the naked Mexican were placed in the circle of howling Apaches and hurried along on foot, followed by a part of the band on foot, while some rode the burros and made sport as they pierced them with the points of their spears and shouted in triumph their victory over the three Mexicans.

Arriving, after a half mile travel, upon the banks of a little stream, lined on either side with a dark, heavy growth of timber, the band halted. A short consultation was held, but the captives understood not what was to befall them, when directly a tall, erect Indian, the lines of whose face indicated some degree of compassion, stepped forward with spear in hand, advanced slowly towards the naked Mexican and then hesitated. He seemed to be unsettled. He soliloquized: "In that man's veins flows the same blood that courses in mine. My father was a Mexican. I can not kill him."

He turned and handed the spear to another Indian, upon whose face savage hate and cruel bloodthirstiness had plowed its furrow deep and lasting. With devilish delight gleaming in his eye he stepped forward, eyed the Mexican with eager pleasure for a moment, then suddenly springing upon him he thrust the spear entirely through his body. As the spear was withdrawn, and the blood spurted forth, the Mexican sprang forward, forced his way through the band of howling Apaches and leaped like a deer down the bluff to the creek, but ere he reached the water's edge his quivering body was filled with arrows. With a wild wail of despair he lifted his hands toward heaven and fell full length at the water's edge. Joaquin was dead. This was an awful scene to Andrés and Pedro, and haunted them in the visions of the night. They knew not how soon theirs would be the like fate.

III

A Vain Pursuit.

It was now noon. The force of wheat threshers had ceased work and were at dinner.

"I must go now," said Don Juan Martínez, "to see the little boys and carry them some dinner. Pedro deserves to go hungry for his disobedience, but I suppose he is hungry enough by this time to eat in spite of a guilty conscience. I shall hurry back, but let the threshing go on in the meantime. It is only two miles over there and I shall be back directly. I may have some difficulty in finding them, however, for I know not the exact grazing grounds to-day."

Martínez hurried on and soon came to the little valley. He discovered the cows standing under the shade of a large oak at the far end of the valley a half mile away, and of course expecting to find the boys near there, he rode in that direction. Disappointed in his search, he began to call, but no answer came.

"It must be," he said, "that they have gone for water to that spring yonder." He waited awhile, then started in search. As he rode across the valley, to his surprise and horror, he discovered the tracks of moccasined feet. He shouted out, calling in wild despair. He followed the tracks out to the road, where he found the flour scattered from the sacks of the Mexican.

"The Indians have stolen my poor little boys," he exclaimed, as the truth dawned upon him fully. "Curses on them," and putting spurs to his horse he sped home, to gather sufficient force and follow the Indians in hot pursuit.

There was consternation in the Martínez family, and in the whole community, when the news of the little boys' disappearance was received, and soon preparations were made to follow the marauding band of Apaches. Some delay was occasioned, however, and by the time the force was fully organized and equipped night was settling down, and it was thought not advisable to start in pursuit till morning, lest they be caught in ambush by the wily Apaches.

No sleep closed the eyelids of Juan Martínez and the family that night. It was a night of heart sorrowing and weeping; a night that seemed never to end. But morning dawned at last, and the party was out and on the trail of the Apaches. They found the tracks of the little boys at the spot where the savages ran upon them. Following on they came to the scene of the capture of the Mexican and his burros. From here they found a plain trail, and soon came upon the mangled body of the murdered Mexican lying full length at the brink of the little creek where he had been so horribly pierced with spear and arrows the evening before.

Following the trail on in the direction of Las Vegas, they came to a stream, but after crossing it, the savages had so adroitly covered their track that no trace of them could be found, and thenceforth all must depend upon conjecture as to the direction the Indians had gone. The party, however, continued pushing forward in the direction of Ft. Sumner, till they arrived at that place, hoping that, while they had lost the trail of the savages, they might still hear from the lost boys through the occasional bands of friendly Indians that visited that point. They waited here for several days, but hearing nothing and giving up hope, Juan Martínez, with tired body and broken heart, turned his face toward home. He never recovered from this awful shock but after three years of anxious search for the little boys through all the savage tribes of the Southwest, with broken heart he died.

~

IV

The Flight.
Little Pedro's Death.

Let us return to the little captives. Leaving the dead Mexican at the creek, in too much haste to scalp him, the Apaches hurried on a few miles towards Las Vegas and hid among the rocks in the hills near Hot Springs. The boys dared not make a noise, and they could only sob in silence.

Poor Pedro! how his heart smote him when he thought of having run away from home that morning. How he yearned once more to hear his mother's tender voice, look into her loving face, receive her forgiving kiss, and feel the presence of her loving arms about him again; but he was destined to see her no more till they should meet before the Father's face up yonder. Andrés tried to comfort him, but the hope held out to him was too vague; it brought no comfort. Night settled down, and the Indians came out from their hiding place among the rocks and underbrush of the mountain side, and stealthily made their way towards Las Vegas, crossed the river near by and found a hiding place in a thicket, not far from the sleeping town.

Here they held a consultation, and leaving four men with the boys, the whole band scattered out in different directions. This is their plan when they go out to steal horses, but when they go out to kill, they stay together, if they have any idea their foes are gathered at any point in numbers.

It was a long night with the little boys. It seemed that the light would never come again. They were confined each between two savages, who threatened them with cruel torture every time the least audible sob or cry was heard from them.

"Shall I ever see home again?" thought Andrés. "When the morning dawns, will father come for us? Will the morning ever dawn again? Oh, I want to go home, I want to see mother. Surely I can go back home to see my mother." And all the long, dark night the boys sorrowed as no one can describe.

In the first early dawn, the Apaches began to return from different directions as they had departed, but all mounted on good horses, and leading four extra horses intended for the four men who had been left with the boys. Here they waited but for a moment, for they knew they would be pursued as soon as the light of day revealed their maraudings. The four Indians sprang upon the backs of the extra horses brought for them, and the two who were the boys' captors seized them with rough hands, pulled them upon their horses behind them, passed a rawhide rope around their bodies, and tied them securely to their own bodies to prevent either falling off or any possible escape in the thick jungles through which they must pass in their flight.

Passing out through the thick undergrowth down to the river, they recrossed, and to deceive any who might follow as to their real purpose and destination, with rapid movement they bent their course eastward, and by daylight were out on a broad prairie.

After a few miles the band, turning their course to the southwest, in sweeping gallop, went thundering along, never daring to stop, lest the people, aroused and in hot pursuit, should overtake them upon the open prairie, where they would be no match for the white man or Mexican. It is only in the brush or among the rocks that the Indian becomes a match for other people. He will not fight in open prairie, if he can avoid it, and out on open prairie, one man behind his horse, or other object, can keep many Indians at a distance. In the brush or rocks, however, he is the superior of all others.

At sunrise, the band went like a whirlwind, thundering down into a beautiful little vega, or meadow, where several thousand sheep were grazing. Spying the poor shepherd, who, on account of the elevation of land to the westward over which the Indians were coming, was not apprised of their approach till they were between him and the little rock fortress just on the opposite side of the meadow, they let fly at him a perfect shower of arrows, many of which fastened themselves into the poor man's quivering flesh. With a cry of despair he fell forward upon his face in apparent painful death.

Just at this moment a report was heard, a whizzing missile, sent from the rifle of a man in the little rock fortress, stayed the purpose of an Indian, who was just in the act of scalping the dead man as he lay there upon his face. But the Indian, behind whom Andrés rode, coming up, and seeing the body of the poor shepherd lying there filled with arrows, sticking out like the spines of a porcupine, shot one more into it, then resolved on recovering some of them. Urging his horse up near the bleeding body, he reached down, took hold of an arrow and pulled; but the steel point, with reverse barbs, was too securely imbedded and fastened in the man's body to be easily extracted. He pulled again, but with no better success, this time lifting the body from the ground as he tugged at the arrow. The next effort was to make his horse stand with his forefeet upon the body to hold it down while he again pulled at the arrows, but this too was ineffectual, and the Indian, seeing that he was being left far behind his fleeing band, gave up the effort and hastened on.

Continuing eastward for a few miles, the Apaches suddenly turned to the southwest. All day long they continued at a rapid rate. Night coming on, they slackened their speed, but did not stop. They had been in too many marauding, murdering expeditions to be caught sleeping. The night travel only would measure the distance between them and whoever should pursue them, if only their pursuers could once get their trail correctly.

The poor little boys were tired and worn, and from sheer exhaustion their heads would droop in sleep, to be awakened in an instant by the abrupt, irregular gait of the horses.

"Andrés! Andrés!" cried little Pedro, as in the flight they came close to each other, "Andrés, I want to go home, I want to see mother, will I ever see mother again! Oh, Andrés, I am so tired. I am—"

"Hush, Pedro," said Andrés, "I can not help you now, and your cry only hurts me the more. Don't call me again."

And here the Indians, in mock tenderness, called out, "We are taking you to see your mother, we know she is crying for you now." And the whole band laughed at the grim, tantalizing joke.

The weary night passed away at last, and the second day dawned; but its rich and mellow light brought no joy to the little boys, for the Indians again increased their speed, being fully persuaded that they would be followed in hot pursuit, and as yet they had not traveled through country where they could well cover their trail. All day long they continued their southwest course. Knowing the country, they kept out of sight of all habitations, lest being attacked and engaged in fight they should be delayed, and then overtaken by their supposed pursuers.

The day passed, night again settled down, but still no halt was called. The long night wore away in travel, and the morning of the third day came, clear and bright, but doomed to be a day of darkness and sorrow to the boys.

Pedro was completely exhausted, and could not sit up. He was crying piteously. He and Andrés both rubbed by the saddles in front, cut by the ropes around their bleeding bodies, and bruised and sore by the constant jogging and irregular gait of the horses, were suffering untold agonies. They had eaten nothing since the morning they left home to herd the cattle in the little *vega*.

Pedro could go no further. He fainted away in his agony, but revived again and continued to cry piteously. The Indians stopped suddenly. A hurried and earnest consultation was held, when the Indian behind whom Pedro rode sprang from his horse carrying the little boy with him. The little fellow could with the greatest effort only stand upon his feet, strained in every limb, heartbroken, dying. Taking a spear from his belt, the Indian, standing behind Pedro, with a murderous grunt, thrust it through the body of the little sufferer.

Andrés, seeing this horrible performance, and forgetting his own sufferings, with a quick jerk at the rope around his body, freed himself from the Indian to whom he was fastened, sprang with surprising adroitness from the horse and caught his little nephew just as he was falling pale and lifeless to the ground. An Indian at this moment urged his horse forward, struck Andrés in the forehead with the end of his spear, inflicting a wound which leaves its scar till this day, caught him by the hair of his head and threw him to his place again on the horse. Quick work this was, and the Indians resumed their journey in a gallop.

Poor little Pedro's body was left alone upon the broad prairie, far away from home, to be eaten by the wolves by night or dried into a mummy by the winds and sun by day. No ghostly marble pointing to the pale and pitying stars shall mark his resting place. The resurrection morn alone shall find him. He sleeps alone till then.

The purpose of the Indians was to reach a timbered and hill country, where they felt sure that pursuit would either be impossible or easily evaded. Yonder to the south, among the rocks and the low, stunted growth, they felt sure that they would be secure for awhile at least. So they pressed their way in that direction eagerly, till reaching the summit of a hill they halted. Here they scanned the country around in every direction to see if there was an enemy in sight. Being assured there was none, they prepared to tarry here till their horses were rested, and they themselves were refreshed. The horses being too much jaded to run off, were set free to graze upon the rich prairie grass growing in profusion everywhere.

But one of the horses must be slain to appease the hunger of the starving Indians themselves. A pony, looking less able to endure the hardships of further travel, was selected, when two Apaches dropped to their knees, drew their bows, and with sure aim sent their arrows to the horse's heart. In a moment the starving Indians gathered around the dying pony, and with butcherknife and dirk, cut off the quivering flesh in great hunks, threw the pieces upon the fire, and scorching them a little began eating with an eager relish, which only a savage appetite could know.

"Little boy, who wants to see his mother, come here. Eat. Good," said Andrés' captor, as he handed him a piece of the scorched, but still bleeding horseflesh. "No," said Andrés, as he staggered back in disgust. But the Indian struck him a blow with his quirt that nearly prostrated him, for already he was weak and bleeding from cuts and bruises received the past few days along the way. Great pieces of skin and flesh hung down from various parts of his body.

"Eat," repeated the Indian, as he raised his quirt for another blow. Andrés took the piece offered him, bit it reluctantly at first, but in a moment his appetite was awakened, the gnawing of his stomach responded, and he began to eat with as much apparent relish as his savage captors.

When Indians suspect that an enemy is upon their trail, they never halt in lowlands or open prairie, but always seek some high point, commanding a view of the surrounding country. At such a place they can rest and watch at the same time. At this time they were so guarded, and here they remained till their horses were rested and they had about consumed the one they had killed. When they again took up their journey, feeling that danger of pursuit was about over, they traveled more leisurely. Reaching the Pecos River they found a great herd of cattle, deserted upon their approach by the herders, grazing along its banks, a large number of which they collected together and drove away for beef as soon as they should reach their camp, only a few days journey now to the west.

V

Andrés' Sufferings.
Resolves to Die.
Engages in a Deadly Conflict with the Apache Boys.
Is Rescued by the Kiowas.

Twenty days had now elapsed since the capture of the little boys near Las Vegas. They had been days of horrible scenes and fearful sufferings to Andrés. Hardly a spot upon his body that was not bruised and bleeding. Great pieces of skin hung from his arms and shoulders. He wished for death. He envied Pedro his sleep back upon the prairie. He longed for a spear through his own heart to end his sufferings. Then the memory of home and home associations came like a flood tide upon hearth and soul. Mother's sweet face and loving voice, father's prudent reproof and kindly advice, and even Dionicio and Regordio's occasional jokes, all crowded the heart and memory almost to bursting.

"Shall I never see them again?" thought Andrés. His heart was breaking, and he resolved to die. He determined to do something to make the miserable Mescaleros murder him. Here was the Pecos River. This would be a good place. They were about to cross it again. This would be his opportunity—but just at this instant there was heard the strange, weird mingling of female voices in the distance up the river. The noise died upon the breeze, but in a moment it came again, louder and yet more near.

The band of Apaches listened for a moment, then raising the triumphant war-whoop dashed forward with all possible speed, for they recognized in the wild song coming to them on the air, the voices of wives and mothers and sisters, who, being notified by a messenger sent ahead several days before, had come a day's journey to meet the triumphant warriors returning with scalps and captives. Instead of greeting first their returning husbands and brothers, the squaws ran upon Andrés, four of them striking him each a blow across his bruised head and bleeding shoulders. There is a peculiar honor and privilege accorded to the squaw who first strikes a captive, and a little less honor to the next, and on to the fourth, after which there is no special inducement to strike a captive but wanton cruelty, which is often indulged in by the squaws, to which, as we shall soon see, Andrés could testify. After the assault upon him and abuse, they turned to pay their respects to husbands and brothers in the returning band.

Soon they were moving forward again, carrying before them the herd of cattle stolen the day before. Again crossing the Pecos, they push their way along its banks, till yonder in the distance, close at the mountain's base, could be seen an Indian settlement. Their camping place was in sight. It was home to them. Indians have no definite abiding place, except as civilization closing in around them forces them to a local habitation. Their wigwams or tepees are only temporary structures, made of skins or ducking, that can be taken up and moved on short notice. When left free to wander, as in the days of these events, they camped only a short time at a place, never more than a few months, often less than a week. But this camp had been established two months before by this band of warriors for the benefit of their women and children, when they started out on their marauding expedition into New Mexico. They were instructed to remain here until their return, as it was a secluded place and secure against an enemy's approach undetected.

The camp was in a stir as they saw the returning band approaching. A wild, savage shout from both the warriors and the campers made the surroundings hideous, and Andrés' heart sank in despair as he thought of his possible destiny. But this time they paid but little attention to him. The squaws took the horses, staked them out by the long hair ropes, or rawhide lariats, led their husbands away to their tepees for rest, while the young men surrounded the cattle and began to kill them, till more than a hundred lay prostrate upon the ground. The squaws came out, and with shouts of joy and songs of triumph dressed the beeves. Fires were built and soon the feast began.

The names of the captors were on all lips, and a discordant song in their honor was made for the occasion, while each Indian of the marauding band was bragging about his own achievements. Andrés was placed in the center of the circle and ridiculed and used as sport for the wild, exultant savages. After cruel jest and wanton sport, for the howling crowd continued till night, Andrés was given over to his captor's wife, a little lame woman, who seemed to have some little spark of human sympathy left in her heart. It is often the case that only suffering will bring one into sympathy with other sufferers, and now the little lame woman was the only one in all that crowd who showed any feeling for the little captive. She took the exhausted boy by the arm and led him along with such kindness that his bleeding heart was to some extent encouraged and refreshed. He was placed into a little cowhide tepee and fell exhausted upon a bed of straw and longed to die. He fell asleep, however, and awakened, not till the bright light of the morning peeped in upon him. He was alone. How strange the surroundings! He lay there and gazed at the shelter over him. He had dreamed of home and mother. He could not realize where he was; but as full consciousness returned, he remembered all the fearful experiences of the past three weeks, and became fully aware again of his surroundings. He had never slept in a tepee before. It was made of two cowhides stretched over the mature stems growing from the center of the yucca plant. Sometimes three hides are used in this way. The wealthier Indians use three or more hides. These hides, either buffalo or beef, are dressed on both sides, and are made as pliable as ordinary tanned leather.

Andrés was not allowed to remain undisturbed long. He was soon called out and given the refused beef, after others had eaten their fill. He soon began a life of servitude, carrying wood and water, and tending the horses on the range; but he was closely watched, and not allowed to be long alone. It was an almost hourly occurrence for the Apache boys to gather around him and hoot and jeer and throw stones at him, 'til his body was covered with bruises and festering sores. This made life unbearable, and he again resolved to die. He made up his mind to go into a desperate conflict with the Apaches and thus die fighting them. He resolved to do this the next time he was sent for water to the spring at the foot of the hill, for it was when he went to the spring that the Apache boys tormented him so.

At the tepee the little lame woman protected him, for she, among them all, seemed to be the only one who had any spark of love or human kindness left in her soul.

At this time Andrés' captor put him to digging a hole in the ground. After digging it about two feet deep, and about the same in diameter, the Indian took a cow skin and lined the hole with it, so that it would hold water. He then filled it with water and mixed into it a considerable quantity of pounded mesquite beans, covered it closely, built some protection around and then left it alone. Andrés became interested in the performance, and watched to see what could be the object. He forgot his sufferings for awhile, and for several days the Apache boys for some reason did not trouble him, except by jeering him as he passed along.

One day, about a week after this, there came to the camp some visiting Apaches from another settlement up the river. The little lame woman was sent out to the hole dug in the ground the week before, and she came in with a vessel filled with mesquite beer, a liquor upon which the Apaches often got beastly drunk. After having drunken freely of this intoxicant, Andrés was, as he thought, traded to the visiting Apache for a quantity of liquor. The little lame woman pleaded for the privilege of keeping him, but to no avail, and Andrés was forced to take his place in another camp under new hands.

But he did not remain in his new quarters long before he was again traded or given to another cruel Mescalero, and here his sufferings began anew. Night and day he was tormented by his persecutors who took the greatest delight in seeing him suffer. One night the chief of this new camp stood out in the dim light of the camp fires, and in a wild, weird voice began to call. Andrés could not understand what he was saying, but as he saw the people coming together he imagined that they were devising some new method for torturing him, and his heart sank within him. But as he anxiously watched, he discovered that the Indians, painted in most fantastic style, were gathering around a tepee down near the creek. Before the tepee a few paces, was a large cedar branch standing stuck in the ground. The Apaches, keeping time to the tom-tom beating within, circled around the tepee three times, then bowing toward the rising sun stooped and entered.

The tom-tom, the rattle gourd, and the discordant song began in earnest, and the Indians were indulging in a Mescal revelry. While they were thus engaged, Andrés had a night of rest, for all night long the tump, tump, tump of the tom-tom, and the noise of the rattle gourd and the singing continued, and when the sun came up and their revelry was ended, they lay down in stupor and slept. When they awoke orders were given to break camp, and in half an hour they were on the march to find a new camp at some more propitious place.

Two months had now elapsed since reaching the Apaches settlement at the foot of the mountain. They were in a land of other marauding tribes, and scouts were kept constantly in advance. One day the scouts in turning a bend in a little valley were suddenly confronted by a band of marauding, warlike Kiowas, their old enemies. They were too close to make any effort to escape, so they proposed terms of peace, and offered to conduct the Kiowas back to the Apache camp, for the full band of Apaches had not that day taken up the march. The Kiowas, well knowing the treachery of the Mescalero Apaches, prudently declined to be led into any trap that might be laid for them, and so to secure safety for themselves they took two of the Apache scouts, placed them under guard, and sent two of their own warriors with the remaining scouts to the Apache camp to have the terms of peace agreed upon and confirmed.

The sudden and unexpected appearance of the Kiowas so deterred the Apaches that it was not long before the matter of peace was confirmed and the scouts had returned answer to the Kiowas.

"The Kiowas are coming," said an Indian to Andrés, "and they will get you."

"Anything in preference to what I am now enduring," thought Andrés; and in spite of his surroundings a faint smile came upon his face, the first perhaps since his capture. Soon the Kiowas came in sight, and although terms of peace had been agreed upon, they went through the Apache camp with some degree of insolence, and seemed to be intent either in provoking them to war or in showing them their superiority; but the Apaches were too prudent to resent it, and endeavored to take everything in perfect good humor.

After the excitement had somewhat worn off, and the Indians of both tribes had nearly all gone to their respective camps (for all had camped close around), Andrés was sent to the creek for water. He fell in again with his tormentors, the Apache boys, and one of them striking him, there began a desperate fight between him, single handed, and half a dozen Apache boys. He struck one of them a blow upon his head which felled him to the ground, and springing upon him, he was in the act of dealing a deadly blow with a stone he held in his hand, when a missile sent from the hand of an enraged Apache struck him a severe blow on the arm. His hold on the struggling Indian beneath somewhat relaxed, and the weapon fell from his other hand, when suddenly, he was hurled by a quick movement of his writhing antagonist to the ground himself. The howling Apache boys rushed forward, and Andrés thought now the end is come, when to his surprise, they began suddenly to scatter and run and in a moment all had disappeared down the steep bluff near by.

Looking up Andrés discovered two Kiowas standing near, who had come upon the scene just in time to save him from the cruel torture of the Apaches. "*Tagnoe akonte*" (Apaches no good), said one of the Indians, as they stood there with spears in their hands.

This was a strange tongue to Andrés, and he wondered what new trouble had come to him now, as he watched them in their feathers

45

and paint and wild paraphernalia. But one of the men spoke to Andrés in Spanish, seeing that he was a Mexican. He himself was a Mexican, captured long years ago, when but a boy, and raised among them, and in ways and habits and dress was scarcely distinguishable from the real Indian.

"Little boy," said Santiago, for this was the supposed Indian's name, "why are you here, and where did you come from?"

"The Apaches stole me from my home about two months ago," said Andrés.

"Is this the way they treat you?"

"Yes; they have nearly killed me several times, and this time I thought I would fight till they killed me and so end my sufferings, for I had rather die than be tormented every day as I am."

"You were giving them a good fight," said Heap O' Bears, who caught what Andrés was saying, although he understood but little Spanish, "and we are sorry that you could not have scalped the crowd, and could we have got our hands upon them we would have scalped them for you. You are brave and now I want to take you from these Apaches and give you to my daughter to be her son in place of her own little boy who died not long ago. You see yonder tepee? To-night, after everybody is asleep, you slip out and come there and I will conceal you. The cowardly Apaches dare not undertake to go into my tepee, and after a few days I will take you across the Pecos River and you will be safe. My daughter will love you and you will be happy with her. Go, now, and when night comes and sleep closes the eyes of the Apaches, you come." All this was spoken in a mixture of broken Spanish and Kiowa, but Andrés was so intensely concerned that with a little assistance from Santiago, he understood all that Heap O'Bears had intended.

"*Sabe?*" said Heap O'Bears as he was turning to go. "*Sí Señor*," answered Andrés quickly, for hope of better times sprang up in his heart, and he was ready for any emergency to bring about this end.

Heap O'Bears and Santiago disappeared down the bluff over which the Apache boys had gone so precipitately a few minutes before, while Andrés, with much apprehension, went back to the Apache camp. News of his encounter with the Apache boys and the interference of the Kiowas having reached the camp ahead of him, he received another horrible beating, but he endured it more patiently, for he felt sure that he would soon make his escape from their cruel hands, and he longed for the night to come. But the Apaches had been watching, and suspected that their enemies, the Kiowas, would seek to steal him, and when the time for sleeping came they placed him close behind an old Indian who was to guard him. He lay very quiet for some time, but at last, feigning sleep, he rolled away from the old Indian, who, with a savage grunt, reached over, struck him and pulled him back.

For a long while Andrés did not move again, till the deep breathing of the Indian assured him that he was asleep, and this time he rolled away from him an inch at a time till he had gotten back against the tepee wall. Fearing he could not step over the Indian without waking some one, he reached his hand out under the tepee covering, and pulling up a stake that held it down, he lifted it, making a sufficient opening through which he could roll. In a moment he found himself lying out in the darkness of the night, prone upon his back, looking up at the pale and pitying stars. But he had no time to indulge the memories of home and mother and loved ones as they came crowding him and choking him as he endeavored to suppress them. Without even rising to his feet he slipped along upon his hands for some distance. When he was at a sufficient distance, as he thought, to be secure, he arose to run, when he was, to his astonishment, suddenly confronted by an Indian, who rose up before him from behind a large stone lying beside the narrow trail.

"*Bueno muchachito, mucho bueno,*" (Good little boy, very good). And to Andrés' great relief he found it was Santiago, who had been watching for him to come, and together they hurried away to Heap O'Bears' tepee.

After partaking gratefully of jerked buffalo meat, prepared for him by Hon-zip-fa, Heap O'Bears' wife, Heap O'Bears said:

"Little Mexican boy—"

"Wait," said Andrés, "my name is Andrés."

"Umph! Andele," said Heap O'Bears, for he could not frame his Kiowa tongue to say Andrés. And Andrés, the Mexican, now becomes *Andele, the Kiowa.*

"Andele," he continued, "I have decided to buy you of the Apaches to-morrow, and if they will not sell you, we are determined to fight for you and take you anyhow. You go back to-night, and to-morrow

47

if a fight begins, you may know the trouble, and you watch your opportunity and come to us. We have no love for the Apaches anyway, and if we take their scalps it will be good. Be quiet and patient and we will get you, if not by trading for you peaceably, we will get you anyhow."

With full instructions, Andrés with anxious heart went back to the Apache camp, lifted the hide covering of the tepee and rolled back into his place behind the old Indian just as he was beginning to wake, and so close was Andrés lying, that the old Indian never suspected that he had been out at all.

~

VI

Sold to the Kiowas.
Becomes the Adopted Grandson
of the Chief, Heap O'Bears.

Andrés had, by the night's experience related in the preceding chapter, become so excited that he lay awake till late thinking of the coming morrow, when he hoped deliverance would come to him. He at last feel asleep, to be awakened abruptly by some one jerking him from the pallet upon which he lay. It was in the broad light of the morning, and he waited with anxious heart for the Kiowas' proposed trade.

At last, Heap O'Bears, having arranged everything for whatever emergency might arise, approached the Apache camp. Santiago was with him, and when Andrés saw them approaching he could hardly conceal his emotion.

"Heap O'Bears has come," said Santiago, "to ask you to sell him that little boy you have there," pointing at Andrés as he addressed the Apache chief.

"How much?" said the Apache.

In answer Santiago led forth a little black mule, and down in front of him he threw two buffalo robes and upon them a bright, new, red blanket.

"He will give you these for the boy," said Santiago.

The bright, red blanket caught the eye of the Apache, who had never before beheld a thing so attractive to him.

"May be so me swap," said the Apache, speaking in broken English.

"Boy, you catch 'em. You give me mule, buffalo, blanket, good." So saying, he turned to his squaw and directed her to take the mule and robes to their proper place, while he drew, with much delight, the red blanket over his shoulders. The squaw objected to the trade, but to no avail, and with a scowl of disapproval she thrust him from them with a force that Andrés never forgot. This was the woman who first struck him when he was carried captive towards the camp at the foot of the mountain. She saluted him with a blow then, she bade him adieu with a blow now.

With a glad heart leaving the Apaches, Andrés was soon established in the affections of the Kiowas. Hon-zip-fa took him to her heart at once, kind and loving as a real mother. She prepared him a dish of jerked beef and raw liver.

"Andele," she said, "your head is sore."

"The Mescaleros beat me and made my head sore, and my body is sore, too. But now I will get all right. You are good to me," replied Andrés.

"Ta-quoe a-kon-te" (Apaches no good), said Hon-zip-fa, as she drew Andrés down upon her lap.

Taking a butcherknife, and scraping it back and forth over a stone to sharpen it, she proceeded to cut Andrés' hair. She carefully worked at it until she had trimmed it close to the scalp, matted as it was with the sores. Having finished this, she dug up the root of a yucca plant, or soap weed, which grew near by and proceeded to make a wash for his head, and soon she had it well cleansed. Hurriedly making him a suit of buckskin, after the Indian fashion, she dressed Andrés up, and he felt like a new creature.

49

Such a change from oppression and cruelty, to one of comfort and kindness, made Andrés very grateful and took his mind at last from thoughts of home. In a few days his head was well and the great sores on his body had healed up, and Andrés was happy and contented with his new friends. As son as he was cared for and dressed in the regular Indian paraphernalia, the Kiowas broke camp and started on to continue their marauding expedition with the purpose of so shaping their course as to reach their home, away to the northeast on the Washita, in early spring.

Heap O'Bears was riding a white mule, and taking his new son behind him led the van. He gave Andrés a good bow and quiver filled with arrows, and very carefully and assiduously taught him how to use them. After the first day's travel, coming upon a herd of horses and mules, Heap O'Bears captured a beautiful Spanish mule, quick and sprightly, which he gave to Andrés. Hon-zip-fa took a cow hide and shaped it upon a crude saddletree that she had made, and thus constructed a saddle for him. He was now equipped for traveling in as grand style as his adopted grandfather.

The Kiowas went on to the southwest, between the Pecos and Rio Grande rivers. Turning across the high land of that region, they soon reached a section that was for many miles destitute of water, and for three days they suffered agonies from a burning thirst. Reaching a rough and rugged section, they came upon a herd of wild cattle, but being so thirsty no one felt disposed to disturb them; but seeing the cattle gave assurance of water near.

The way being so rough it was difficult to ride over it, Kankea got down from his horse and started afoot in search of the water that he knew must be near at hand. In spite of their suffering, a wild shout of merriment went up from the band when they saw Andrés leap from his little Spanish mule and start out, keeping abreast with Kankea, and sometimes ahead of him.

"*Ziddlebe, Andele, ziddlebe, kataike,*"[1] they shouted.

Reaching the summit of a little hill, the two discovered, lying in a little valley below, a most beautiful lake of water, reflecting from its clear and placid bosom the blended hue of verdant earth and azure

---

[1]Brave, heroic Andrés, good, very good.

sky. Never was a sight more welcome—nor more beautiful. Never was there a more intense physical agony than that of a burning thirst; never was there a more grateful sight than a fountain of living water to slake that thirst. So in the spiritual world. The agonizing wants of the soul are met by that fountain of living water springing up unto eternal life.

With a wild shout of delight, and a wave of the hand to the deployed band, Kankea and Andrés rush down the slope to the edge of the lake, fall prostrate and drink till they could hold no more. Then sitting up, Andrés fell over deathly sick, while the water ran from his mouth and nose and eyes. Soon recovering, he drank again, and at last felt quite relieved. In a moment, the whole band, horses and men, were at the water's brink and in the lake, and soon all were revived.

After reconnoitering the vicinity, it was decided to camp for awhile somewhere near the lake, and go out on a horse stealing and plundering expedition. Andrés, two men, and Hon-zip-fa were left in charge of the horses and the camp, while the others took lariats, bows, and quivers well filled with arrows, and started out on foot in search of horses. When Indians go out in search of scalps they ride their fleetest horses, but on a horse stealing expedition, they ride their slowest, laziest horses, and if they hope to find them near, they often go afoot.

Andrés and those left behind made their camp about four miles from the lake, lest other marauding bands, coming for water and discovering them, should fall upon them. But one of the band, from a hidden place, kept watch each day over the lake to see who came there and to give warning of any approach in their direction. After night settled down they would drive their stock to the lake and take the pack mules with the water jugs each day.

Their water jugs were made of the beef or buffalo paunch. When a jug is needed, a beef or buffalo is killed, the paunch is taken out and cut open, the rough inner lining is removed, the paunch is dried, and the edges are pinned together with smooth, wooden pins, which bring it together, looking, when filled with water, very much like a large, short-neck gourd. Two of these are filled with water and placed across a pack saddle and carried sometimes long distances.

After a week the Kiowas began to return, but without any horses, looking defeated and forlorn. Their "medicine" had failed them. There was something wrong. They waited in silence for the return of the rest of the band. Several days more passed, and yet Heap O'Bears, Big Bow, Napawat, and Santiago had not returned.

The band grew uneasy, but continued to wait. Two more days passed away with increasing anxiety, when, just as the sun was dropping out of sight and the Indians were preparing to "make medicine" to ascertain the fate of their comrades, they hear in the distance the wild, weird song of coming victors. It was the song of triumph, discordant and wild as the howling of demons from the lost world. An answering shout went up from the camp, and strange as it may seem, the missing four came in from different direction, each bringing in a considerable herd of horses. Instead of a night of mournful worship, as had been intended, the night was passed in wild feasting and savage joke.

~

VII

Kiowas Reach Home.
The Big Medicine Dance.

After a day's rest, the band broke camp and started for home. It had now been more than eight moons since they started on this expedition, and it would take not less than two moons more to reach their home, away to the northeast on the Washita. Bending their way as expeditiously as possible, they came, after several days, to Rock River. A big snow had fallen and it would be slow traveling for a time. A consultation was called one morning, and it was decided as they were now out of probable danger from pursuit or attack from an enemy, and there was none between them and home, that those who could travel faster should go on in order that their people, who must by this time be getting quite uneasy, might know that all was well. Heap O'Bears, Stumbling Bear and To-hor-sin, the three chiefs, with the larger portion of the band, therefore hurried on, but left sufficient force to bring on the stolen stock. Andrés and Somtottleti were put in charge of Heap O'Bears' horses, and, both being Mexican captives, soon became fast friends and remained so ever after. Pai-ti drove Big Bow's horses.

After traveling slowly along for several days, one day, reaching the summit of a rise in the prairie, they were confronted by a vast herd of buffalo. Stretching northward as far as the eye could reach, the whole prairie was black with them. They had not been hunted enough to be wild, and the Kiowas drove unnoticed right into their midst. For days they traveled surrounded by the buffalo. They killed several every day before halting for the night, and cut out choice pieces of the flesh for cooking, but always consuming the liver and kidneys raw, with a portion of the paunch and entrails before leaving the carcass. These were always considered choice and delicate bits.

It was the custom among these Indians from early spring till July, to kill buffalo to get their hides for tepee covers. The hair was too short for robes, but later in the season, when the hair was long and nappy, they killed them for the purpose of making robes of the hides and storing away the meat, while it was fat for the winter. For a small tepee, about eight buffalo hides were used. For the ordinary size, twelve were used, but sometimes the head chief used as many as twenty, thus making a very large tepee, or wigwam, twenty-five or thirty feet in diameter. These hides intended for the wigwam are dressed on both sides by the squaws. They scrape off the hair on the outside, and the inner, fleshy lining on the inside by a tedious process with bone instruments manufactured from the larger bones of the buffalo or beef. Later, when they could get iron, these instruments were made of iron. It took much labor and a long while to dress the hides in this way, but when done, they were as pliant as any leather manufactured after our most improved process. The hides intended for robes are of course dressed only on the inner side but they are made very pliant and comfortable.

When a boy or girl grows up to sufficient size and age, a *Pa-lo-tle-ton* is set apart for his or her exclusive use. This is a buffalo robe, neatly dressed, made of a full skin, with the head fastened by the lips to the head of their lounge-like, willow beds. The young people, the boys especially, enjoy special privileges and attentions when they are fifteen or sixteen years of age. They have their own way and they control the household. The *on-ta-koi* is the ordinary robe for the bed. It is only a half robe, and cut off also at the neck. The hide for the pa-lo-tle-ton is carefully taken off, with all the skill of the taxidermist, so as to preserve the full covering of the head, with even the horns and eyes and ears and lips, and also the legs down to the hoofs, and sometimes even the hoofs are retained.

After many days' travel through the buffalo, the band had secured enough hides to supply the fullest demand for wigwams or tepees, for every pack mule or horse was loaded down and could carry no more.

Nearly three months had now elapsed since the Kiowas had started on their homeward march, and they had reached Red River, which they crossed where now is located Quannah, Texas. They had encountered, during all this time, no one, save a band of friendly Quojale [Quahada] Comanches. After crossing Red River, they pushed on more rapidly than before, and soon reached the Washita, where their people were camped. The squaws seeing them approaching, rushed out to meet them and raised the war cry, as was their custom when a band of warriors was returning home. All was strange and wild to Andrés, but he felt perfectly at home, as the Kiowas had been very kind to him and given him all the rights that belonged to one of their own number.

There were a great many tepees in this camp, and Andrés was anxious to see on the inside, as he had never yet been in one intended for a whole family. But first he started to unsaddle his little mule, but a squaw pushed him aside and unsaddled the mule herself. Andrés looked at her in astonishment, and was about to resent it, when he discovered that the squaws were attending to all the stock, both unpacking and hobbling them out upon the prairie. This was the Indian custom, but not according to the polite Spanish manners taught him by his mother. He submitted, however, and turned to enter a tepee, when another squaw pulled him abruptly back. This time he felt offended and made some resistance, but the squaw was too much for him and he had to give up. He went, however, to Santiago to know why he was not allowed to go into the tepee.

"Pull off your quiver and other war implements," said Santiago, laughing. "No warrior is allowed to enter a peaceful home with accoutrements of war and plunder on, and you look too warlike."

This speech made Andrés feel very much larger, but he soon divested himself of his quiver and warlike bow, and, together with Santiago, entered a tepee. The bow and quivers and buffalo skins were all turned over to the squaws, whose business it was to keep everything at hand ready for use.

Andrés watched everything with profound interest, and he took on the Kiowa ways very rapidly. Opportunity was soon given for becoming a convert to their superstitious worship, and engaging in their dissipating amusements, for they had been in camp only a few days when, suddenly, he discovered the whole camp in a stir and commotion. The tepees were all taken down, and, together with the blankets and buffalo robes, were rolled up and placed upon the pack horses, while the tepee poles were tied at one end, half a dozen on a side, to a rope around the neck of a pack horse, while the rear end dragged upon the ground. In a remarkably short time the whole camp was deserted, and the whole band was on the march. The time of the annual dance had come and they were getting ready for it, and since the return of all the warrior-bands without hurt, they must worship and make sacrifice to their idol gods, lest they be angry and give them no further success.

Grand preparations were going on. Heap O'Bears had made a circuit of the tepees of the whole Kiowa tribe, for it was to be a grand occasion. It was the custom for the chief "medicine man," when the time of this annual worship drew near, to hang his "medicine" or idol around his neck, tie a representation of it to his saddle, and circle every tepee whose occupants he wished at the dance, and all those who were thus circled were bound by every sacred obligation to go under threat of heavy penalty; for if they refused to attend, some great disaster would be visited upon them by the idol during the year. If any tepees are left out by the medicine man in his rounds, either by accident or with intention, the inmates were sure to suffer great evils during the year.

The medicine chief, before starting out on this circuit, always paints himself white from head to foot, and the only garment he wears is a buffalo robe thrown over his shoulders. He neither eats nor drinks till he has circled all the tepees, unless it takes more than four days, in which case he is at liberty at the end of four days to stop on his way and build a "sweat house" and worship, and then partake of food and drink, after which, being refreshed, he goes on his journey till he has circled every tepee of his tribe.

It may be interesting here to tell what a "sweat house" is. It is built of slender poles, usually willow, about two inches in diameter, which are stuck into the ground in a circle about six feet across, and then bent together at the top and tied, thus forming a dome-shaped structure, which is covered with buffalo robes and blankets, making it as near air-tight as possible. This makes a tepee, or medicine house, about four or five feet high. The ground on the inside of this booth is covered with a thick coating of prairie sage gathered around here and there on the prairie. This plant the Indians have special reverence for as having special and mysterious powers, and it figures very largely in all their superstitious worship. In the center of this medicine, or sweat house, a hole about six inches deep and a foot in diameter is dug. The "medicine man" takes into this place his idol, or medicine charm, a bucket of water, and an eagle feather fan. The eagle feathers are also held in special reverence and are supposed to have peculiar power in sickness and in war. Hence they use a bunch of eagle feathers over the sick in their superstitious rites, and their war bonnets are made of eagle feathers.

Rocks are heated in a fire built near the sweat house, and then taken and placed in the hole in the center. The chief medicine man with all the worshipers goes in, the robes are tucked down securely, so that no heat can escape, and but little air can get in. The bucket of water is then poured upon the hot rocks, and the worshipers lie down or sit around in a cramped position. The steam arising from the seething rocks soon causes the perspiration to pour off the worshipers in great profusion, when their weird incantations begin. No one is allowed to use a fan till the chief medicine man has gone through the first act of worship, calling all the while upon his grandfather, *"kon-kea, kon-kea, kon-kea,"* in continued repetition, accompanying his voice with the well-timed motion of the eagle feather fan. It would be a sacrilege to use any other kind of feathers. After this first act by the chief, all the others may begin chanting and fanning and calling upon their idols and their dead ancestors. After this sweating, worshiping process is through, the worshipers make whatever offering is required, and the worship is ended.

The sweat house is used also in case of sickness without the worship. The sick person is placed in the booth, the water poured on the hot rocks, and when the pores of the skin are expanded, and the perspiration is pouring from every heated opening, he rushes out of the sweat house and plunges into the river. This either kills or cures. In some cases it cures, in many it kills.

The "medicine" of which mention is so often made, is the idol or image that the Indian worships. This consists of a little rock image with its face painted with a solid coat of yellow, and on this yellow background are alternate stripes of red and black drawn down in zigzag course, radiating from eyes and mouth. This image, when the Indians are not on the march, is hung up on the back of the tepee in a sack of buckskin made for the purpose. On the inside is another similar sack, hung on the west side of the tepee, containing scalps, paints, rattles, medicine charms of various kinds, which superstition has led them to gather from time to time.

After the medicine man has made the circuit of all the tepees and has returned to his own, the Indians break camp, and, gathering from all directions, come together at one place. This was the grand move that first attracted Andrés' attention after reaching his adopted home.

On this first move, Etonbo, Heap O'Bears' daughter, who afterward married Zilka, took Andrés to her home and bosom to be her son. He lived with her till the death of Heap O'Bears, and she was ever kind and affectionate as a mother to Andrés.

After the tribe had all come together and settled down, the four chief medicine men got together, made an offering of some kind and then selected a tree, straight and sleek, which was to be cut for the post around which to dance, and to which they were to tie the buffalo. The order was as follows: They select a good level place near the timber and water. The medicine men then return and send out messengers to announce that the place has been selected, and all things are ready. But if no place has been selected, it is so announced, and another effort is made by the medicine men going through the same form of worship as before. But before the medicine men make this second effort, the whole camp must move to another place designated by them. At last, when a place has been decided upon and so announced, the dog soldiers get together, paint their faces and bodies, shout out the signal, beat their tom-toms, and make the surroundings a perfect pandemonium. On the next day, the crowd, ready and excited by this time, begin their approach towards the consecrated spot selected for their worship. The chief medicine man leads; his wife, carrying the chief idol, following close by his side. The captive Mexicans come next and then the twelve chosen medicine men follow with signs and symbols of superstitious worship, and at the last the great multitude, with the dog soldiers on either side as out riders. They go a certain distance, then halt and worship. This is repeated four times, and at the last halt an old Indian, noted for his age and wisdom, steps forth and announces to the crowd, expectant and eager, that when the word is given, the first one who reaches and knocks down yonder pole upon the consecrated ground, nearly a mile away, shall be endowed with special privileges and honors, and peculiar blessings shall come to his band of dog soldiers during the year. As soon as this announcement is ended, and the signal is given, a wild, mad, tumultuous rush is made in reckless abandon as to personal safety, or the safety of anyone else.

There are four honors, the first one reaching the pole taking the chief one, and the others in the order in which they come. After this rush is over, the circle is formed. Within the circle at the west side is located the "medicine tepee," into which the idol image is carried, and in which the "medicine man" remains the four days of the dance. Early next morning a captive Mexican woman, accompanied by the dog soldiers, is sent out to cut the tree that has been selected. They approach the tree, halting and worshiping four times before reaching it; then the Mexican woman strikes one blow with the axe and stops, when she and the soldiers again sing and pray; then another stroke followed by worship, and on till the tree is cut down. The dog soldiers then rope the tree, and by the four-fold method of approach and worship carry it to the grounds and put it into its place in the center of the circle. While this is going on, the great crowds are gathering together poles and limbs of trees and, with much enthusiasm, completing the arbor for the dance.

It takes about four days to complete the whole arrangement. When everything is ready, those who dance go outside the circle, strip themselves of all clothing except the breech clout, paint their bodies white, dress in a buffalo skin, and finally go in, making the noise of the wild buffalo bull. They circle around the medicine man's tepee four times, then go back to the entrance of the large circle, then to the entrance to the arbor around the center pole, circling this arbor four times, each time motioning to enter, but not entering till the fourth time.

They then take their places in the dance circle. The medicine man steps forth from his lodge, circles around four times, as did the dancers, and entering, hangs the idol upon the pole, and takes his place in the lodge behind the idol. The musicians go through the same performance, and take their place near the entrance, just inside the lodge. The musicians begin their monotonous music with tom-tom and rattle-gourd, when the medicine man steps forth, perfectly nude except his buckskin breech clout, the ends of which are drawn up before and behind through a panther skin belt around his waist, and, hanging down between his painted legs, keep time in resultant motion with the movements of the medicine man and the wild freaks of the prairie winds. His body, instead of being painted white, as the common dancers, is painted yellow, while his feet are painted black. Bunches of prairie sage are tied to his wrists and ankles, and he wears upon his head a jack rabbit bonnet. In one hand he carries a bunch, or fan, of crow feathers, called the 'Tsine-ke-ah-lah, and in the other, a whistle made of an eagle bone.

He goes up to the image, takes into his mouth, as he worships, a bit of root of some wild plant, grinding it in his teeth, turns to the circle of dancers and goes round spitting and blowing it out upon them. He next takes his eagle-bone whistle and runs around the circle blowing it with all his might. He goes through this performance four times before the way is open for the common dancers. The eager crowd then begin their wild performance, singing, leaping, yelling, praying, till out of breath. They then rest a while, but soon begin again. They stare at the image, hooting and howling in the wildest manner, then at the sun, in a wild, foolish, fixed, idiotic stare, and cry out, "Yes! yes! now our enemy is blind. He can do us no hurt. We will take his scalp and steal his horses, and we will be secure."

The medicine man, taking the 'tsine-ke-ah-lah, or crow fan, calls the attention of the dancers, runs around the circle several times himself, then in wild gyrations whirls the 'tsine-ke-ah-lah around and around, while the dancers, fixing their gaze upon it, try to keep eyes and heads in harmonious movement with the motion of the 'tsine-ke-ah-lah, till dizzy and exhausted many of them fall prostrate upon the ground in apparent unconsciousness, hypnotized.

Thus they lie for a long time, and often profess to see visions that indicate their future destiny in life. If an Indian, during the year, vows that he will dance before the idol, and doesn't do it, some sure calamity will befall him. An Indian arose one day in a camp-meeting being held by the Methodist missionaries and began wailing. After a little while he stopped suddenly and began to talk. "I vowed," said he, "that I would come here and cry before your God, for I believe he is strong and can help me, and now I want to keep my promise and fulfill my vow; for I have had much sickness and the Indian medicine (or idol) has failed me. I want to turn to the white man's God, for he is strong." And then he continued wailing, thinking that was the correct way to get the ear of the white man's God. He was endeavoring to carry out the ways of superstition in the worship of the true God. He wanted to pay his vow. He was afraid not to do it. He was taught the way of God more perfectly, and soon after professed faith in Jesus and joined the church.

While all these things were going on, Andele was looking on in astonishment, learning rapidly the Indian ways and absorbing fast the Indian superstitions. He watched Heap O'Bears, and wondered how it was possible for him to do so many wonderful things. He listened to the crowd of howling dancers and watched them as they leaped around in their nakedness before the idol. It was all wild and weird to him.

VIII

The *Quo-dle-quoit.*
Andele has a fight.
The Scalp Dance.

The big dance was at last over, and the Indians broke up and scattered abroad. But before breaking up, on the last night of the dance, all those who expected to go out on the warpath, or stealing and plundering expeditions during the year, gathered around a buffalo rawhide, took hold of it with one hand, and with small sticks in the other beat upon it, while they called upon their idol to help them and bless them, thus:

"O, *Kon-kea-ko-on-to*, O, Grandfather, blind our enemies while we creep upon them, keep them asleep while we plunder them, help us to get many scalps and captives, and steal good horses, and don't let us get hurt."

And thus they went on beating the rawhide, singing and marching and praying, till satisfied with the performance, they broke up to start out in small bands to the various fields of plunder and murder. The men who did not intend to go out on these raids during the year were not allowed to go through this performance, for it amounted to a pledge to join in some marauding expedition.

The Quo-dle-quoit constitute a privileged class among the Kiowas. It is an honor or privilege that is transmissible, and no one can be Quo-dle-quoit longer than four years, when a successor must be selected. Each Quo-dle-quoit selects his own successor, who must of necessity accept the honor and submit to be painted after the manner of the Quo-dle-quoit, which is as follows: Around the forehead, at the edge of the hair, are parallel streaks of black, and these are continued around the face and drawn down under the chin. On each cheek bone is the picture of the moon very far advanced in crescent.

61

On the center of the chest is the picture of the sun, and on each side of the chest, a little lower down, is again the crescent, painted in dark green, shading out into a very light green toward the open side of the crescent which is turned upward. The sun on the chest is also a light green, but the whole body has a coat of solid yellow as a back ground to all these other ornate colors.

The Quo-dle-quoit wears a jack rabbit bonnet, ornamented with the ears of a jack rabbit and with eagle feathers. Instead of *painting* the sun and moon on the chest, they are often *cut* into the flesh, leaving for all time to come great sun- and moon-shaped scars. When one is selected as a Quo-dle-quoit, and, according to custom, is painted up and ornamented, he must pay his predecessor well for it, and each year as his predecessor paints and ornaments him, he is obliged to pay an additional installment of ponies, blankets, robes, etc., for four years, when his Quo-dle-quoit ceases. He must then in turn transfer it to some friend and receive remuneration from him in like manner as he had to give to his predecessor.

This works oppressively sometimes, but no one dare refuse to become a Quo-dle-quoit when once selected. The Quo-dle-quoit never looks into a mirror of any kind. He dare not see himself. He is denied the privilege of eating dog, or polecat, or of being around the fire when cooking is done, or enter a tepee where a dog is. There are many other things denied him, but he enjoys security in war. No weapon of war can hurt him; he is secure.

The morning after this first big dance the men all scattered abroad in various directions. Andrés was left with the women. They had all learned to like him. At the first he was kindly received. His adopted mother had made some clothes for him, even before he had reached the Kiowa settlement. Santiago's wife, who was Heap O'Bears' sister-in-law, carried him first to her camp. He felt free and did as he pleased. He was the adopted grandson of the chief, and he had been instructed to resent any attacks made upon him by the Indian boys.

During Heap O'Bears' first absence, he suffered somewhat from the boys who had become jealous of him on account of the favor shown him, a captive, but he soon had an opportunity of showing them that he was able and ready to take care of himself. It was during a scalp dance after Heap O'Bears' return. He had been gone about two months when he returned with two scalps, that of a negro and a Ute Indian.

The scalp dance is a grim performance and generally lasts about three weeks, and they dance night and day. No man is allowed to dance who was not in the fight when the scalps were taken. But all the women are privileged to dance. If no scalps are taken, or one of the band is killed, no dance is held; but when they return with scalps a grand jubilee is held. When a successful band is approaching home, they slip up stealthily until near by, when suddenly they raise the war-whoop and charge upon their own home, which creates a panic till they are discovered to be friends instead of enemies, and instantly a responsive war-whoop is given by the wives and mothers, and preparations begin at once for the dance.

They hang the scalps upon a pole, while they go dancing in a circle around it, singing and beating the tom-tom, and all the while calling in tantalizing jeer to each of the dead men: "Poor fellow, he tried to save his life, but look at his scalp! He cried aloud, but we only laughed. We shot him through the heart. He fought hard, but we overcame, and his scalp looks beautiful hanging there. Our medicine made him blind while we killed him."

While going through this performance they constantly shout out the praises of the men who took the scalps. They are the heroes of the occasion. In all this wild, weird performance the squaws show the greater fierceness and devilish joy.

After the dance is over they offer the scalps to the sun, or sometimes to some particular idol to which they had made promise before going out to war. When they make the offering to the sun (or some idol), they pray: "O, Sun, give us power, to get other scalps. Give us long life and make us brave chiefs. Keep our enemies blind and deaf so they will not detect our stealthy approach." Often they keep the scalps to tie to their medicine charms and to grace their belts.

At these scalp dances the boys are allowed the fullest liberty, and encouraged to take part in, and enjoy, the hideous performance. It was at this scalp dance, upon the return of Heap O' Bears, that Andrés gave evidence of his purpose to defend himself. While the dancing was going on one night, he and other boys, dressed in buffalo robes, were running through the circle and jumping over the fire in the center and bellowing like a mad buffalo, when suddenly he and Pakea collided as they met in the center. They both, with bruised heads, fell backward. After they had recovered from the shock, and were on the outside of the circle, Pakea, while Andrés was not aware of his intention, or even of being angry, struck him a blow that nearly felled him to the ground.

He arose with all the fire of his Spanish blood stirred to the utmost, and began a fight that must decide his standing among the Indians in the future. If he was overcome by Pakea, then he would be the butt of ridicule and contempt and imposition. But if he overcame, he would stand as a respected chief among the boys, and be an object of admiration among the old people. Indians have great respect for the one who wins in a fight, whether the winner be of their own race, their friend, or foe, and so this fight meant much to Andrés. He was determined to win, and so he put his whole heart and muscle into it, and in the very first onset he struck Pakea such a blow as caused a wail from him that indicated the result at once, and when the Indian dancers, who had suspended dancing for a moment to look on, saw what the result was, they cried out, *"Ziddlebe, Andele,"* that is, "brave and dangerous Andele." Some touched him on the breast and on the back muttering out some exclamations of approval and admiration. It was a victory that became an epoch in his Indian life. From henceforth he had no more trouble.

If an Indian band who has been out on a marauding expedition returns without scalps, there is no dance. If one of the number has been killed, there is wailing and lamentation, and very soon the chief who was leading the band must go in search of the tribe or people who did the killing and get a scalp. If he fails, he must very soon go again, and again, till he succeeds. He goes to the spot where his comrade was killed and begins his search. He paints his face a shining black, something like a stove polish color. He throws away his mourning apparel, and goes forth, not as a mourner, but as a proud warrior. In carrying out this principle of retaliation one can readily see why the Indian tribes were in constant or continuous war with each other.

On a certain occasion, Andrés, with a considerable band of Indians, obtained permission from the government agent at Anadarko to hunt upon some of the unoccupied lands of West Texas. While they were there hunting a company of Texas Rangers came upon them, killed one of their number, scalped him, cut his finger off and left him. The Indians hurried back to their own reservation, stated to the Indian United States Agent what had occurred, and demanded of the agent that they be permitted to go again to Texas and kill a Texas man in revenge. Whether the agent through fear for his own scalp gave his consent, it is not known, but the Indians did go and in a little while returned with the scalp of a hated Texan, held a big scalp dance and were satisfied. After an Indian has been killed, the daily mourning is kept up till scalps of the enemy are secured, and then the mourning ceases.

~

IX

Heap O'Bears is Killed by the Utes, and is Scalped. Somtotleti Dies with Him.

Three years had now elapsed since Andrés had been stolen near Las Vegas. It was the spring of 1869. Andele had become a veritable Indian with but little trace of civilized life left in him. He had learned many things of the Indian life, and had accepted them all. The annual sun dance had been held, when Heap O'Bears, with his band of Kiowa dog soldiers and allied bands of Comanches, Arapahoes and Cheyennes, started westward on an expedition against the Utes, against whom Heap O'Bears, on account of past offenses, had a "bad spirit." He hoped, with the aid of his allies, to give them a blow from which they would never recover.

Passing on westward after three days' travel, and coming to a mountain pass through which ran a small mountain stream, a fierce bear, with swift gait and seeming fright, came towards them from the windward, and circling around them passed out of sight down a mountain gorge. In a moment every Indian drew rein and sat in silent awe. For sometime no one spoke—all seemed to apprehend that a dread calamity was before them. Finally Heap O'Bears broke the silence:

"Now, we started out under 'strong medicine,' surely we are not to be forsaken by our god, but what means that *Tsaitim* (Bear) crossing our path to the windward, and lifting himself as if in warning of future doom if we go forward? But it can not be, for the medicine was good, the signs were right. The medicine said, 'go, kill Utes.' We will go forward."

"Hold," said the Comanche leader, "your 'medicine' is broken. For some reason the wind blows you down and it sends the Tsaitim here from the windward to warn you, and whatever be the 'medicine' you trust, the matter has been given over to other hands, and you dare not go forward. If the bear had passed on the other side of us, and had not raised those warning feet of his, you would, with us all, have been safe. But you know what it means when a bear crosses a warrior's path to the windward."

"Umph! Umph!" sanctioned the respective leaders of the Arapahoe and Cheyenne bands.

"I dare not go back," said Heap O'Bears, "lest I disobey and insult the 'medicine' that assures me aid in all my wars, and thus suffer punishment at his hands. I will defy this new, and doubtless evil omen, and go on any how, but if you people are afraid, I will let you return, and I will go alone to scalp the Utes. The squaws will doubtless entertain you upon your return, and help you to dance around the scalp of a jack-rabbit instead of a Ute."

Heap O'Bears spoke this with much earnestness and sarcasm, but at the same time betrayed some apprehension on account of the dilemma he was in. The Comanche leader straightening himself full in his saddle, and while his eagle eyes in proud gaze stared upon Heap O'Bears, made answer:

"We are here, Heap O'Bears, as you well know from conflicts with us in the past, behind no one in courage and in readiness to scalp the Utes, but the Tsaitim indicates that your medicine is broken and your doom sealed should you go on, and we do not wish to see your scalp taken nor to feel ours jerked from our heads by the howling Utes. We can do nothing when the power of the medicine under which we go is destroyed."

Heap O'Bears sat awhile in deep thought and finally spoke, "As leader of this expedition, I feel the weight of responsibility. I would not see you murdered through my mistake at the hands of the Utes. Let us camp here till another sun comes up, perhaps new light will come with it. This night I will go alone out upon the mountain yonder, and consult the medicine and pray for direction, and what I receive shall be for our guidance."

"Umph! Umph!" and approval came from the allies.

So the whole band moved down upon the little creek to camp for the night and wait developments. As night came on Heap O'Bears painted himself white, having washed off the black war paint, gave instruction that no one come near him during the night, went out upon the mountain side and there remained alone all night till the early sun began to peep over the eastern hills, when he came in with a revelation from his medicine. All listened with deep silence as he spoke.

"I must go back home," said he, "and start again after a short rest and a sacrifice to the medicine. Let the whole band await me here. Seven suns will see me back again."

"But we must all return," said an Arapahoe.

"No, no!" said Heap O'Bears, "for I find the sign was for me and affects my people alone, and it is only necessary for me to return."

He was reluctantly allowed to go alone. The band waited patiently till the evening of the seventh day and as they saw the sun rapidly sinking in the west, they began to grow anxious. Their fears were soon relieved, however, for just as the last lingering beams of the sinking sun were kissing a departure to hilltop and boughs, Heap O'Bears from a mountain pass came suddenly in sight of the place of encampment.

"Heap O'Bears comes ready for the Utes this time," said he, as he neared the camp and alighted from his horse. The allied bands all received him with gladness and on the next day they broke camp and moved on westward. After a hurried and continued march of three days, they descried a band of Utes on a hill some distance away watching them, and while they were consulting what to do, to their surprise there came from another direction a band of Utes sounding the warwhoop and eager for the fray. Before the allies could recover from their surprise, the Utes were full upon them. The allies whirled into line, confronting the Utes, when suddenly both sides halted, and sat upon their horses gazing into each others faces, neither side speaking a word nor otherwise breaking the silence for some while; when at last a young Kiowa raised his spear and struck a Ute full in the face, and cried out as he did so:

"If by striking the first blow upon a hated Ute I become chief, then am I chief now, for the deed is done."

This was the signal for a general engagement, and in a moment a dozen lifeless forms, pierced by arrow and spear, lay full upon the ground. Desperate was the fight. The Utes seemed to know no fear. They were upon their own territory, and their homes were at stake. They closed in upon the Kiowas. The Comanches were panic stricken and fled. The Arapahoes and Cheyennes who were farther to the left, seeing the courage and desperate fighting of the Utes, did not venture to the help of the Kiowas, but kept at safe distance. Heap O'Bears, becoming separated from his band, was surrounded and pressed upon every hand.

"I shall die here," he said. "I can fight, but I can not run and here will I pay the penalty of my foolish distrust in my medicine by turning back when I should have gone on. Let my braves leave me to my fate and save themselves."

The band was rapidly retreating, when Somtotleti learned of Heap O'Bears danger. He rushed back, and declaring his purpose to die with his friend and chief, he forced his way through the band of Utes and stood beside Heap O'Bears, who was already bleeding from several wounds. He shot one Ute from his horse, and then another, and still another, and the Utes were about to give away, when they discovered that Heap O'Bears and Somtotleti had no more arrows. They rushed upon the two helpless comrades with renewed fierceness and hate, filled their bodies with arrows and scalped them while they were yet gasping. When this was done the Utes looked to find the allied bands, but they had retreated to a safe distance, and were fast making their way towards the rising sun again. Thus this war was ended.

X

Mourning for Heap O'Bears.
Horrible Sight.

Ten days had passed since the battle with the Utes and Heap O'Bears' death. Night had come on, and the fierce prairie winds, with renewed force, were howling mournfully as they swept through the village of tepees, or wigwams, at the foot of the bluff near the Washita, located there till the braves should return from the Ute war. In much merriment, Andele and the Indian boys had been going through with a mimic performance of "medicine making," and he had at last lain down upon his bed in the west side of the tepee.

All was quiet. He was not yet asleep. He was, perhaps, indulging a faint thought of the home from which he had been stolen, of the mother upon whose loving bosom he had so often been pillowed to sleep, of the scenes that he had encountered since he had last seen her, of little Pedro's cruel death; then of the Indians' wild dance, of the discordant songs to which he had listened, and wondering, still wondering, he had dropped into a half conscious sleep.

His memory had taken up the whole chain of events, and was passing them before his mind like a panorama in vivid colors, tracing in rapid succession from this to that, when a thousand painted faces, hideous and wild, stood before him, and suddenly a wild wail mingling with the mournings of the western winds as they swept over the far-stretching prairie, came like lamentations from some lost soul wandering from the regions of the dead. He sprang up in horror and trembling from head to foot, stood speechless.

After a little while, recovering himself, he concluded that it was only a bad dream, and that it was but the night wind howling around the wigwam. He was just in the act of lying down again, when once more he heard the strange, wild wail, this time coming nearer and nearer and more distinct. Heap O'Bears' wife awoke, listened a moment, and then throwing up her hands, began howling in accord with the noise of the seeming demoniacs approaching in the darkness of the night. Andele was nearly dead with fright, but he soon found out that it was the band of warriors who had gone to fight the Utes under Heap O'Bears. They were returning without their chief, who was left lying back upon the prairie, scalped by the Utes.

In a moment Heap O'Bears' wife gathered up a whetstone and a butcherknife lying near, stripped herself perfectly nude down to the waist, raked the knife back and forth over the stone, and then began cutting herself. She cut her arms from the shoulders down to her wrists, and gashed most horribly her breasts, and then smeared upon her face the blood that gushed forth from every wound.

Andele was horrified as he gazed upon her there in the dim light of the cotton wood fire. Heap O'Bears' wife, not content with cutting her arms and breasts and smearing the blood upon her face, placed one of her fingers upon a rock and asked a friend to chop it off. And there she stood, bleeding and howling, accompanied with the howling of all the camp in such discord as can be portrayed only by emblems drawn from the world of fiends. All night the howling went on, and next morning as the sun came up, a great fire was made of all Heap O'Bears' personal property and a number of ponies were killed for his use in the happy hunting ground. He was a chief and great honor must be done to his memory; and besides, he must have a chief's full equipage for the hunting grounds beyond.

~

XI

War with the U.S. Soldiers. Cheyennes Surprised in a Scalp Dance.

According to Indian custom, Sunboy, who was Heap O'Bears eldest brother, in a short while married Hon-zip-fa, Heap O'Bears' widow, and Andele went to live with Napawat, Heap O'Bears' successor. Here he found it very disagreeable, for Napawat had two wives and they were frequently in quarrels, and Andele suffered from their contentions, as he undertook to serve both.

Mourning for Heap O'Bears was kept up all year, at sunrise and at sunset of each day, till the next spring, 1870. When Indians are mourning they go out some distance from the tepee and stand with faces toward the sun as it rises or sets and howl most pitifully.

At this time Napawat, with a large band of Kiowas, was camped near the borders of the Cheyenne reservation, and just across the line the Cheyennes had scalped a white woman, and were holding a wild scalp dance, while Andele, with other Kiowas, was still mourning for Heap O'Bears. One morning, about three o'clock, the whole surroundings rang out with the crack of rifles in rapid succession The soldiers from Ft. Reno had stealthily surrounded the Cheyennes for the purpose of capturing them, but when they saw that they were holding a scalp dance around the scalp of the white woman, it so enraged them that at once they began killing them. Andrés, with Afpoodlete, rushed out and caught the horses hobbled out on the prairie, the squaws packed up and they started down the Washita River as rapidly as possible. Andele and Afpoodlete were ordered to go with the squaws, but as soon as they had started them well on the way, they slipped back and went with the band to the scene of the conflict.

When day dawned the soldiers had disappeared, but the battle field, or rather the slaughter pen, was a scene of horror, that gave Andele no good opinion of the white man or his God. Here were Cheyenne men, women and children, slaughtered and lying promiscuously in the snow stained with their own life blood. A woman with her lips burned off, stiff and cold, was propped up against a tree, a horrible, grinning spectacle. Men and women perfectly nude were placed in such positions as would not be proper to describe here. This was done by the civilized soldiers of a Christian land, to mock the barbarous savages of heathen tribes. Which is worse,—the civilized (?) soldier, or the brutal savage?

This sight enraged the Indians and a yell of revenge went up from them as they looked on. The Kiowas and Comanches from every quarter began to gather to aid their friends, the Cheyennes. They were preparing for the attack next day, but the soldiers, who were in camp a few miles away, hearing of the proposed attack of the allied tribes, took up the line of march back to Ft. Reno. The Indians followed, however, and in the attack cut off a considerable troop of soldiers from their command and killed them nearly all.

Andrés, being yet but a boy, was compelled to go back with the squaws to a place of safety down the Washita. As they went, an old squaw discovered near the trail they were traveling a little hollow stone image with both legs and one arm broken off. She snatched up the image, called the hurrying crowd to a halt, held the image out in her extended hand, and began praying, "O good image, O grandfather, give us long life. Never let us grow old. Give immunity in war and success in battle. Make our enemies blind that we may kill them. Give us long life, give us long life, and in it all, youthful strength and beauty."

She then passed the image to the next one in the circle, for by this time a large circle had been formed, with instruction to pray as she had done, especially for long-continued youth and beauty. Each one prayed thus as they worshiped the image till it came Andele's turn. While he believed in Indian superstitions with all his heart, yet as he gazed at that broken image he could see no possible good to come by worshiping it, so, in the spirit of humor and ridicule, he took the image in his hand, extended his arm and began, "O good medicine, O grandfather, I pray to you, I never want to be older and uglier than I am now. I want to be always young and beautiful and never old and ugly like the squaw that started this worship."

He did not get any further with his prayer, for the old squaw in her wrath and the crowd in their merriment broke up the worship in much confusion, and soon all were again on their way.

The soldiers were driven into the fort, but in a few days they started with reinforcements again in pursuit of the marauding Indians. They came upon a band of warriors near the Washita and after a sharp engagement, they captured Lone Wolf, Big Tree and Tsaintanta. Under a flag of truce they called a council with the Indians at which they told them if they would bring in all the warrior chiefs with those on the warpath, that the three captured chiefs would be released, but if not, they would be shot. This was a bitter pill for the Indians to swallow, but there was no alternative, and they were compelled to submit. At this council, therefore, peace was made and the chiefs released.

Gui-pägo or Lone Wolf, principal Chief of the Kiowas, 1866–74.
Jackson 1872, Smithsonian Institution.

XII

Scalping the Utes.
A Grim Joke.

It was now fully spring and Napawat sent an old man out to announce that he was going to start out on a certain day to avenge
upon the Utes the death of Heap O'Bears, and that all who wished to
go under his leadership must be ready by that time.

The dance was held, the band gathered around the rawhide, worshiped in the usual way, and at the appointed time, started westward

in search of the Utes. They reached the Ute country about forty miles north of where Heap O'Bears was killed. Napawat had ridden apart from his band some little distance, watching carefully as he went, when suddenly he spied a Ute watching a deer. He raised his bow and with unerring aim sent the arrow through the heart of the unsuspecting Ute. As he fell lifeless another Ute, before unseen, sprang up from the weeds close by and was in the act of shooting when Napawat thrust him with a spear as he ran upon him, and he also fell.

By this time Napawat's band of warriors came up, but too late to aid in the killing. Napawat scalped both the Utes, but the second one was not killed, but was left wounded and scalped to suffer and slowly die.

Napawat was now satisfied. He ceased mourning and felt jubilant. He started with his band for home at once. Big Bow was somewhere not far away with his band, for they had separated the day before, to come in on the Utes in different directions, but Napawat did not take time to hunt him up and notify him that Heap O'Bears' death had been avenged. He reached home in triumph and the scalp dance began at once. The dance had been going on nearly a day, when Big Bow came in with a Ute war bonnet, quiver and bow, which he had obtained in the following manner: When Napawat killed the first Ute, the Ute's horse, standing near, got away and ran off. Not long after Napawat had scalped the Utes, and with his band of warriors had started in triumph for home, Big Bow, ignorant of Napawat's whereabouts or doings, arrived with another band at or near the same place, captured the Ute's runaway horse, and was moving along slowly and cautiously, when he came upon a Mexican.

"Show me to the Utes, and I will spare your life, and give you this horse," as he pointed to the captured animal.

"*Bueno*," said the Mexican, as he mounted the horse. Leading the band of Kiowas along, he pointed out the wigwam of the Ute who had been scalped, but was still alive.

"Umph!" said Big Bow in satisfaction as he pushed on in the direction of the tepee, while the Mexican, taking advantage of this movement, disappeared down a bluff on the new horse he had so easily obtained. But that horse was destined to give him trouble as we shall soon see.

The Ute who had been scalped was carried as soon as discovered to his tepee. He was a chief, and when his friends saw the Kiowas under Big Bow approaching, they put on him his war bonnet, put a bow and arrows in his hands, and propped him up in a dignified posture, that he might deceive his enemies, and die like a chief, and then, to save themselves, left him, and disappeared down the steep bluff close by. When Big Bow come up, seeing him with war bonnet on and bow and arrows in hand, he supposed he was ready for fight, but quickly found him an easy prey. He stabbed him two or three times, jerked off his war bonnet to scalp him when, to the consternation of his superstitious soul, the scalp was gone! He rushed back, mounted his horse, called to his band, and started in full sweep for home, the thought all the time arising, "where is that Ute's scalp?" He had killed the man, he knew that. He saw him die, but the scalp— unless he could carry back the scalp to grace his triumph and make merry over, what good was it to kill a man? "Where was that scalp, anyhow?" he continued to enquire as he hastened onward.

He reached home just in the midst of Napawat's scalp dance, and after some hesitation told of his venture—how he had killed a Ute, but when he jerked off his war bonnet, and went to scalp him, the man's scalp was gone.

Napawat raised a yell of fiendish merriment that astonished the crowd. He then related how he had scalped the Ute while he was still alive and that he was now dancing around the scalp of the man that Big Bow had so courageously (?) killed. Big Bow, downcast and ashamed, left the dance. Napawat danced on, while he indulged in grim jokes about the man alive with no scalp, and about the brave (?) chief who killed him.

Napawat became a great chief. He took the idol that had been kept by Heap O'Bears for his own. But before he could be secure in its protection, he must undergo the torture, which was as follows: He went to the mountain, into some lonely place where no one would disturb him, painted himself white, put on a buffalo robe with the hair side out, took a pipe, and mixing together tobacco and certain medicine leaves, began smoking and praying to the sun, and making offering to the sun of his own blood as he cut himself in nearly every spot. He neither ate nor drank for four days and in the feverish condition induced by this torture he dropped off to sleep and dreamed.

Before sleeping he smoked to the sun and prayed that he might understand whatever revelation the sun might give him through the dream, whether he was to be a war chief or a medicine chief and what was to be his life mission. The vision of successful war and bloodshed and plunder came before his feverish brain, and when he awoke he stepped forth with proud and elastic tread in spite of his emaciated condition, strong in the conviction that a great war chief was he.

The Mexican to whom Big Bow gave the Ute's horse, not long after was riding the horse along the streets of Trinidad. The news of the killing of the Ute chief had already reached Trinidad where he was well known, but it was not understood that he was killed in war with the Kiowas. Bands of Utes often visited Trinidad, and had made friends with many of the Mexicans and mixed breeds and whites who lived there. That was their trading post at this time.

A band of them were standing near the entrance of a grocery store when they saw the Mexican riding by, and they at once recognized their chief's horse. Had they found him out on the prairie they would have killed him at once, but as it was, they could only make known the matter to their friends in Trinidad. As soon as it was known, the Mexican was promptly arrested and placed in jail. He lingered there a long while and when placed on trial the circumstantial evidence against him was overwhelming, but through some technicality in the law he was finally released.

XIII

Foot Fight. The Indian Worship.
The Sweat Booth. Buffalo Medicine Song.

The Indians during these years wandered from Kansas to Texas, and westward and southwestward to the Rocky Mountains and

Mexico, plundering wherever they went, the numerous tribes as often in war with one another as with the hated whites. They never stopped more than ten days in one place, their wandering depending much upon the movements of the buffalo, upon which they chiefly subsisted. Sometimes in their wanderings, the different bands would get separated, and for more than a year never see each other, but when they got together again, there was general rejoicing and the occasion was usually celebrated by a foot fight.

This is a pugilistic exercise, only the feet are used instead of the boxing glove. The two sides, consisting of from one to a half dozen on a side, stand apart a dozen or more paces, and at the signal given, run toward each other, and, just before meeting, whirl, jump as high as they can, and kick backward with full force. Often one antagonist plants his moccasined foot right into the chest or abdomen of the other and kicks him senseless for awhile. It is often as dangerous and brutal as a pugilistic encounter between Corbett and Sullivan.

Andele became completely Indianized. He took up his time in studying the Indian ways, for he had now come to believe all their superstitions, and engage in their worships. He had caught the spirit of their aspirations, and he hoped to be a great war chief. He thought the Indian idol, or "medicine," would pity him and help him, and so he cried to it, and often at night he would get up, go to the medicine man, worship, and offer a blanket or bit of property he possessed.

At the medicine man's tepee the idol is tied to a pole which is leaned against the back of the tepee, and over this pole is a rope of buffalo hair, tied near the idol and drawn entirely around the tepee. When a worshiper comes to make an offering, he stands outside crying thus, "*Kon-e-ko-on-ta*, Grandfather, help me. I want to kill my enemies. I want to be a great chief. Let me live long, and when I die, let me die the death of a brave man in war."

After he has kept this up for some time, the wife of the medicine man comes out, loosens the rope and lets the idol down. It is enclosed in a crescent-shaped buffalo-skin sack. She takes it and places it on a tripod a few feet just back of the tepee, and then the worshiper goes to it and prays to it directly, after which he ties to the stand or tripod upon which the idol is placed a blanket or other article which he gives as an offering. That offering remains there till next day, when the woman takes it into the tepee and places it beside the "medicine," and after a few days it is put to the use intended. If the offering is a pony, a stick about six inches long is tied to the crescent-shaped sack containing the idol, while the pony is hitched somewhere near by. The medicine man himself goes to the pony, cuts a lock of hair from his head and tail, prays to the sun for a blessing upon the worshiper, and then buries the hair. That pony is a sacred offering, and must never be struck over the head.

Often Andele engaged in this worship as above described, and sometimes in the early morning, after a night of anxiety, he would go and gather poles and build a sweat house, that he might worship in that way. He had heard the medicine chief say, "You have to feed the idol if you get any benefit from him." And so seeking the greatest benefit, he was ready to make any sacrifice.

On one occasion he promised the sun-god to make a sweat house in his honor and worship in his name. He put a squaw to cleaning off a spot, while he himself went to a willow thicket and brought the necessary material for the medicine booth. After the preparations were all made, he went to the tepee of the chief medicine man. After the usual ceremonies he entered, circled around to the left, as is their custom, till he came to the idol, which he untied, and, retracing his steps, walked back to his newly constructed sweat house. He was soon followed by the medicine man himself, who, before entering, looked up to the sun and prayed, then called out, "All who wish to worship here now, come, come, come."

This soon brought together all those who wished to worship at this time. They assembled near the door of the sweat house and stripped themselves entirely nude before entering. Upon entering they all circled to the left, the medicine chief taking his place in the west side facing the east, with the idol lying just in front of him. The long-stemmed pipe, well filled with a mixture of ground sumac leaves and tobacco, which, according to custom, had been placed near the idol, was taken up by the medicine man preparatory to smoking, while Andele stepped out upon the prairie for a piece of dried horse ordure, which he lighted and then took it in a split stick and held it to the bowl of the pipe, while the medicine man proceeded to smoke and mutter some petition to the sun as he puffed the smoke upward. Andele put the split stick down near the fire in the center of the tepee till the smoking was ended.

Just outside, at the entrance to the tepee, was placed a buffalo head with the nose toward the entrance, and a few feet further away was a little moon-shaped furnace with a fire in it. In this worship, after the smoking is over, the split stick is taken and placed upon the summit of this moon-shaped furnace. The rocks are placed in this furnace to heat. The medicine man takes a little tobacco and prays to the sun, to the moon, to the earth, and to the idol before him in the tepee. Four times he goes through this form of smoking and praying to the heavenly bodies and to the earth and to the idol. While he offers the smoke to these idols and motions towards the four cardinal points of the compass, he also prays to his grandfather: "O, Grandfather, give me power over my enemies; make them blind that I may kill them; help me to steal good horses. Give me health and long life."

After the medicine man is through he passes the pipe to the one at his left, who worships and smokes as the chief before him had done, and he in turn passes it to the next worshiper at his left, and so on till the extreme left is reached. The pipe is then passed back around the semi-circle to the extreme right, when the smoking and worship begins again and passes on as before to the left.

The smoking both in worship and in social life is done in this way. A semi-circle of three to ten or even twenty is formed. One of the number lights a pipe, or often a cigarette made of leaves, smokes a few whiffs, passes it to the man at his left, who likewise smokes, and passes it to the left, and on till it reaches the last one on the extreme left, when it is then handed back to the right, and it passes on as before, each one smoking a few whiffs and passing it to his left. It would be a serious breach of etiquette to pass it to the right instead of the left.

It is seldom an Indian ever smokes alone, but he shares the same cigarette or pipe with others. Often there may be only two of them sitting together smoking, but the same rule is observed whether there be two or a dozen.

In the worship, after the smoking is over, the medicine man orders the hot rocks to be brought. The one who makes the sweat house and calls for the worship must go for the rocks. He places them at the door of the tepee, when the medicine man goes through the four-fold mode of receiving them. He worships, then motions as though he would receive them, but does this the fourth time, when he takes them and places them in the center of the sweat house in the little hole prepared for them. Then he receives the water in the same way. He begins to tap upon the bucket with a small switch, and, after motioning to do so four times, he pours the water upon the hot rocks, praying each time as he motions. The steam arising from the hot rocks and water causes the perspiration to pour forth from every pore in great profusion, while the worshipers strike themselves over shoulder and upon back and sides with buffalo tails and grass. They sing some and call upon their dead ancestors, "O, Grandfather, give me success in war, that I may get many scalps and much plunder and never be hurt myself."

If, while they worship, it gets too hot, they go through the fourfold form of worship before raising the tepee to let the cool air in. After the worship is ended they all pass out, filing to the left. If in this worship they hear the voice of a woman or a child, it is a good omen, but they dare not look at themselves in any sort of mirror, nor come near a jack-rabbit, or bear, or other wild animal.

Andele got accustomed to this form of worship. He became an expert and at last ventured one day to try to cure a wounded man whom a Texas Ranger had shot. He gathered with the crowd of medicine men around the man and began to sing the buffalo song. This song is sung only over men who have been wounded. It would be a sacrilege to sing it for mere amusement, or on other occasions than bloodshed. They shook buffalo tails over the man as they sang, and finally one of them cried out, "I feel like my gods are all over me." He slapped his sides, and shook himself, and roared in mimicry of the buffalo bull, and began to spit red paint that he had in his mouth into his hands and rub it upon Andele's face, and say to him, "There, I give you that to make you a great medicine chief." And Andele verily thought that this would endow him with greater power.

When he had, therefore, according to custom for medicine men, tied a lock of buffalo hair to his own scalp lock on top of his head, the man who gave him the paint said, "Go now and dream, and when you have dreamed, return and let me know, and that shall indicate more fully your future strength and power."

Andele at once went away alone. His purpose was to get all that there was to be had from the idols. He had deep faith in the unseen, the supernatural, and fully felt that there was power above that could be transmitted to men, and *would* be in answer to sacrifice and prayer.

And if there was anything that he could do to get this power he felt that he must do it.

Receiving instructions as to how to paint his body, he went to his hiding place in the mountains to dream. In the earnest, excited, almost fevered condition of mind he could not but dream, and so the dream god soon revealed to him that he must secure from the medicine man who gave him the paint a certain shield in which there was great virtue. So going to the tepee of the man, he took down the shield and carried it and placed it on the top of a sweat house he had previously prepared, but carried the idol to the inside.

Sankadotie, seeing the purpose of Andrés to get the shield, tried to dissuade him.

"Why," said Andrés, "do you not want me to get the shield when there is much power in it?"

"Because," answered Sankadotie, "if you get that shield it will prove a great burden to you."

"In what way?" asked Andele.

"Very many ways," said Sankadotie. "Let me show you, for instance; every time you cook you have to place on top of your tepee for the god of your shield a piece of the meat you are about to cook, and if you should forget to do so at first, then you are compelled to throw the whole of it away, for it becomes polluted meat and the anger of the shield's god will be against you, if you go on cooking it."

"But my purpose is to get power, that I may subdue my enemies and be successful in war, and I am willing to carry a burden if I can but secure that," said Andele, as he turned away, lest further persuasion should be used. He went on with his performance to get the shield.

"Here," said the medicine man, "are some crow feathers, deer hoofs and buffalo hair, tie that to your hair for a sure and powerful medicine."

Andele replied, "I will take this, but I want your shield with its powers transferred to me. What can I do to secure it?"

"Here," again answered the medicine man, "take this," and he handed him a long curled lock from a cow's tail painted green, "with this your powers will be increased. When you wish to paint, put this in your mouth and blow, and you will get the paint needed."

"But I want your shield," again Andele replied. He was so persistent that the medicine man seemed to be at a loss what to do, so he said, "You have not paid me enough yet."

Andele had already given him many things, but he was ready to make any sacrifice to get the shield, for he felt he must have it. He went away disappointed, but still planning how he could become the owner of the shield with its powers. Among the young, he often made a display of the powers already conferred upon him by the gift of the paint, crow feathers, and cow's tail. One night he dreamed that to get the shield he so much coveted, he would have to give a white horse, but he had none, and he was unable to get one, unless he went out on a marauding expedition and captured one.

~

XIV

Marauding Expedition into Texas.
Massacre on the Washita.

It was now the opening of 1871. Napawat while on a visit to the military post at Ft. Sill, took sick and lingered, in spite of (or on account of) the skill of the medicine men, till spring. He promised his idol that if he would make him well he would go on a marauding expedition to Texas.

In answer, as he thought, to this vow he was soon able to get out. He then took a considerable band of young warriors, went down to Greer Country to hold a dance, and prepare for the warpath. Andele was quite young, but he determined to go.

"Andele," said Napawat, "you are too young for war."

"No, no," he answered, "I want to go, I know I can scalp the enemy. My medicine is strong."

"If you go," said Napawat, "you will go with me. Come, and while I do not like to take children to war, you may learn something for future conflicts. We will dance around the rawhide and get ready."

Next day after the dance, Napawat and Andele got horses and called together the band and started for Texas. Mokine, Kankea, and

Quo-e-kon-kea, were also in this band, and well had they proven their skill in past conflicts in jerking scalps from the heads of dying victims. The band crossed Red River and went several days journey down into Texas, and finally reached a timbered country.

Alighting for a short rest, they hid their saddles away in the underbrush, and went on bareback for two days. About the middle of the afternoon they reached the summit of a hill from which they could survey the country for many miles around.

Two *villas* were in sight not many miles away. Napawat stood gazing intently toward one of them muttering something to himself, when he discovered Andele close at his side.

"Andele," said he, "you want to be a great chief, and you want to be successful in war and plunder, and now look yonder at the hated Texas man's houses. You shall have an opportunity soon of showing whether you be a man or squaw. If you be brave you shall have all my property at your command, but if you be a coward and play the squaw, you will have to go home and carry wood on your back, and water for the squaws. Very soon the sun will go down and the Texas man with his wife and children will be asleep and know not that the braves of the Kiowas are coming to take their scalps. You must not be afraid either to scalp the hated Texas man or steal his horse."

The indignation rose in Andele as Napawat talked. To be called a squaw is about the greatest insult that can be offered an Indian, and Andele was indignant that Napawat should even intimate that there was even any probability of his being like one. He replied as the fire flashed from his eyes:

"I will never be a squaw. If you don't find me as ready in conflict as any in this band, then you can put me to carrying wood and water and nursing the papooses for the squaws, but I am sure to leave that job for some more woman-hearted warrior in your band."

"Good," replied Napawat, as he looked at Andele's swelling form, for he seemed to grow larger as he made his boast. "A trial of your courage will soon be made," and Napawat pointed again towards the villa at the foot of the hill.

The sun soon sank out of sight and left all in darkness and quiet, save the bustle of the people in the village below. It was cloudy but the moon came up, and, now and then through the rifted clouds shone full and bright. The band led by Napawat, with Andele close by his side, stole quietly and cautiously down the hillside and listening, waited patiently till everything was still and all were asleep.

"Let us keep together," said Napawat, "and break in yonder"—but suddenly the violent barking of a huge dog awakened the inmates of the house to which Napawat pointed, and knowing from this violent conduct of the dog as he sprang forward to the full length of his chain, that there was something unusual, the Ranger grasped his gun and peering out at the window of his log house, discovered the Kiowas as they approached, and began firing so rapidly that the Indians concluded there were many men hidden away, who had possibly learned of their presence, and were fully prepared for them. Without raising the warwhoop at all, Napawat called off his men, but as they passed around between some houses a pair of mule's ears were discovered by Andele sticking out from a stable door.

"If we are to be deprived of the expected conflict and it is to end thus," said Andele, "I will venture to take that mule as a fit trophy of this raid." Springing forward, he threw back the half broken door, cut the rope with which the mule was tied, led him out and just as he was clearing the entrance to the corral, the white man who had fired upon them, sallied forth with rifle, but for some unaccountable reason did not fire. Mokine called to Andele:

"Leave the mule and run, for the white men are gathering. Don't you hear the guns?" and gun answering to gun was heard in every direction. The white men, the Texas Rangers, who were so well organized in those days, were gathering from everywhere, and the Indians had lost their opportunity. It would be a narrow escape if they got away at all.

"I am no squaw," answered Andele, "I may not be able to get a scalp, but I will take back some fitting trophy of this shameful and cowardly retreat, to help you and the squaws carry wood and water, or I will lose my scalp in the attempt," and defying all the danger that surrounded him he pulled that mule along, till the mule, at first reluctant, became frightened at the approach of the Texas Ranger behind, and springing forward kept pace with the horse Andele now rode, for he had remounted. He soon overtook the retreating band of marauders, when he discovered that Kankea and Napawat each had secured a horse apiece.

"We must travel without rest, till the sun comes up," said Napawat, "for the Texas man will be upon our trail with many men by the first light of the morning, and if we wait they will overtake us before we cross Red River back into our own country."

All night long they pushed forward in a rapid gallop, for after leaving the immediate vicinity of the village they were on open prairie, with nothing to hinder their course. As the sun came up again they reached the skirt of the timber where they had hid their saddles several days before. They stopped for an hour's rest, when they saddled their horses and remounted. Early in the morning, after another night's travel, they reached the Brazos River at a very bad crossing, and turning up the river they concluded to recross where they had forded some days before. As they were rounding a bluff near the place of the crossing, Kankea, who was at this time at the head of the band, suddenly whirled his horse around, threw his body down to one side of his saddle, and in the low guttural tone of the Indian exclaimed, "Soldiers!"

The whole band of Kiowas plunged into the river from the bluff and swam to the other bank, when the soldiers, who had mounted as rapidly as possible, dashed up. But seeing that the Indians had crossed, they hurried back to the regular ford and were soon in hot pursuit of them as they swept over the prairie toward the northwest. All the morning the pursuit was kept up, the Indians throwing back defiant signs as they hurried on.

About noon, the soldiers halted; the Indians seeing this rode on a short distance and halted also, for their horses were well nigh exhausted. Had the soldiers known this, they could, by a rapid race, have overtaken them. They rested here for a while, keeping eyes on the soldiers, and then started on. During the night they crossed Red River and camped for a short while near the foot of Wichita Mountains. The next day, having pushed on towards the north, they had reached a place near a little creek north of the Wichita Mountains, when suddenly they were startled by the war-whoop coming from a band of warriors returning from the westward, who had captured a number of horses and taken several scalps.

The taunts and jeers of this band cast at Napawat for his failure to get scalps, raised Andele's indignation so that he did not, as he had intended, tell of their cowardly retreat from the Texas village. He knew that neither he nor any of the band would be allowed to dance or rejoice with the victorious warriors around the scalps that they had taken. He consoled himself, however, when he saw a number of the victors on foot, their horses being so jaded that they were unable to carry their owners. He knew that it was a sure sign that they, too, had been compelled to run before the hot pursuit of the hated Texas Ranger. So it was with a relieved feeling of pride and condescension that they loaned the returning victors a number of good horses that they themselves had taken in Texas.

The victorious band hurried on from here and soon reached their camp, where they held their scalp dance. Napawat with his band turned his course eastward, toward the mouth of Chandler Creek, as they had learned that their squaws and children had in their absence moved the camp to that place.

In a few days many had gathered here, but the band of victorious Indians had gone on towards Anadarko and camped near the agency, where, fresh from their marauding expedition, and flushed with success, they were very insolent and soon had brought on a state of affairs that presaged a massacre. Those near the mouth of Chandler Creek had been notified by the military at Ft. Sill to come in and surrender their warriors, and while they were consulting what to do, there came news that an outbreak had been already made near Anadarko and a number killed. At once the whole camp broke up and started to join their people in the conflict.

Reaching the Washita they crossed the river a few miles below the agency and going up the river they found the agency deserted. Big Bow led his band to the store of the Indian trader, broke it open and plundered it of such things as he liked. He secured a considerable amount of money in greenbacks, from the smallest shinplasters to the larger denominations, and not knowing the value of it made cigarette paper of it for smoking the mixture of sumac and tobacco.

While this was going on, Andele was active in his efforts to so learn the arts of Indian warfare that he might become a great chief. He had been now in so many exciting scenes that he cared no longer for the shield of the medicine man, and ceased his efforts to secure it. When this outbreak at Anadarko (1872) took place, the various military posts were notified, and soon troops from Ft. Sill, Ft. Reno and Ft. Elliott started for the conflict, for it was apprehended that the outbreak would be general and would take many men and much time to subdue it. The Indians finding that the United States troops were gathering from Ft. Sill and the other posts became alarmed and started westward for the Rocky Mountains.

XV

Tahan, the Captive Texan

Once when a band of Kiowas were on a marauding expedition down in Texas, they plundered a frontier home, and murdered all the family except a boy of about five years of age. Him they carried captive away, to be given (for adoption) to a squaw who had lost her only son. The Indians not knowing nor caring for his real name called him Tahan (meaning Texas man), for the reason that he was captured in Texas.

All Indians are named from some circumstance connected with them, and this is why there are so many singular names among them. Stumbling Bear looks like a great awkward bear reared back on his haunches, hence his name. A boy was born about the time the Indians had ceased mourning in a certain camp, hence was called, *Kea-kee* (or Quit Mourning). Another was born at a time when the mother was far away from home, hence he was called, "Born a long ways from home." If Tahan was old enough when captured to know his name, he was too young to give it correctly to the Indians, and hence he at once accepted the name given by them.

At the time of this outbreak near Anadarko, Tahan was about eighteen years old, and was as complete an Indian in habits, customs, and superstitions, as the most extreme Indian, and was as bitter and cruel in purpose of bloodshed and plunder. When the Indians started westward, and had, after a day's travel, reached a point several miles north of the Washita River, they pitched camp, hoping to rest several days before they went on. Tahan seeing what was before them, and remembering that he had left his best horse at their former camp, and that he would need him, started after him. It was about ten miles to the south, but he could go there and get back in time to go on with the band westward.

He had, on some raid, secured a good rifle, and when he reached the crossing on the Washita, on the Ft. Reno and Ft. Elliott trail, he discovered a deer. He shot and wounded it badly, but did not kill it. He sprang from his horse, hitching him hastily with the lariat to a bush, and leaving his gun hanging to the saddle, he ran after the wounded deer, which had fallen some little distance away. He butchered the deer, and returned to get his horse, but just as he took hold of the lariat, a troop of soldiers rode up from the steep banks of the river and took him prisoner. It was a squadron of cavalry going as couriers with papers from Ft. Elliott to the commanding officer at Ft. Reno. They hurried Tahan on before them, not knowing at first that he was a full blood white.

An Indian scout who had been watching the trail saw that Tahan was captured and soon communicated the news to the Kiowas. At once Napawat called the whole band of warriors to mount, and away they went in hot pursuit. In the course of a few hours they came in sight of the squad of soldiers, but just as the soldiers were meeting a large troop coming with a train of wagons from the direction of Ft. Reno.

Napawat, seeing there were too many now to attack openly, decided to try strategy. He turned and went with his warriors back towards the crossing on the Washita, near which was a deep cañon through which the soldiers must pass in traveling towards Ft. Elliott. It was decided that they would conceal themselves there at the summit, and when the pale-faced soldiers were in the cut, they would attack them. Napawat and the band got to the place decided upon, dismounted, stripped themselves, and painted themselves in such a way that they were a hideous sight to behold.

They had not long to wait, for soon they beheld the head of the column coming cautiously along. As they lay in ambush, they watched anxiously for Tahan, for the only purpose they had in view was to recapture him. He was veritably an Indian. He knew not the white man's language. He loved the Indians, and they loved him. Tahan they must have, and Tahan was just as anxious to get back to them.

They soon discovered him in charge of two soldiers, one on each side. Becoming over eager, the warwhoop was raised too soon, for the soldiers had not yet reached the most disadvantageous ground, and when they heard the war-whoop, and saw the hideously painted

Kiowas coming, in quick movement they whirled their wagons around into a kind of fortress, and were ready for the attack.

The Indians seeing the celerity with which this was done, and the accuracy with which the soldiers fired, were deterred, and hesitating awhile, fell back in some disorder. They soon rallied and came again, but were again repulsed. Again and again they charged upon the encampment, but the soldiers had now secured themselves by spade and shovel in throwing up breastworks. Night came on, and the fighting ceased till next day. During the night some of the Indians crawled up as close to the solders' encampment as they dared, and began to call, *"Tahan, Tahan, ema, ema."* (Tahan, Tahan, you come, you come.) They continued to call him, "Run away from the soldiers and come on, your grandfather is waiting for you. He wants you to get him some buffalo meat. Come on." For three days the siege was kept up, each night the Indians calling for Tahan, who was kept under close guard by the soldiers.

Andele all this time was among the foremost in every charge, and several times he made narrow escapes. On the third night the Indians held a council and decided that if they did not accomplish something next day, they would withdraw, and go on their way westward. They had settled on plans for the next day's attack, and had all gotten quiet, when some one in subdued voice was heard calling:

"Where are you, grandfather, where are you? Are you all gone?"

"Listen," said Andele, "who is that? Somebody calls."

All listened with fear and superstitious anxiety; for while it sounded somewhat like the voice of Tahan, yet it seemed to be far away and weak. But again the voice came, clearer this time as it called out:

"My people, where are you?"

"Who is that?" called Napawat.

"I, Tahan. I come."

In a moment the whole camp was in commotion, running together and crying out, "Tahan! Tahan! he has come, he has come," and they threw their arms around him and rejoiced over him.

After sometime all was quiet again. Tahan was telling with much interest to his dusky friends how he had, by rolling out from under the blanket under which he was lying, slipped away and made his escape in the darkness, and he supposed the soldiers who were guarding him had not yet detected his absence. While thus engaged they discovered just there in the darkness, slipping stealthily along in their direction, the form of a warrior.

In a moment every man grasped his spear, for they thought it the approach of the enemy, and they were ready for the conflict. But they heard someone speak in the Kiowa tongue. Napawat called, "Who are you?"

"Umph," grunted back the voice. "Your friends have a hard time to find you, Napawat," for it was one of his own band who was left several days before at the river crossing to watch that, and who had come to warn him of danger.

"You need to be quick. If you have accomplished nothing here, it is too late now, for soldiers are coming from the way of the setting sun in great numbers. The whole earth is covered with them, and they are camped to-night not far from our squaws and papooses, and are headed right now towards their camp, and to-morrow our squaws and papooses will all be murdered, as were the Cheyennes not far from here not long ago, unless something is done quick."

Napawat listened until this speech was through, then called out to his men to mount, saying, "If we be men, let us put ourselves between the squaws and papooses and danger. Let us die like brave men should die, rather than see our children murdered and our women outraged as were the Cheyennes." Every man in the whole band gave the grunt of approval, and soon all were on the march.

The soldiers knew not that the siege was raised till next morning. They ventured out cautiously and soon found that the Kiowas had all disappeared. Where, they knew not. Could they have known, there would have been no need of caution as they broke camp and continued their march. As it was, they marched slowly and with every precaution, lest the Indians should undertake another ambush attack.

When Napawat reached the camp of the women and children in the early morning, he found that the soldiers coming from Ft. Elliott had camped not far away, and that now what was done would have to be done quickly. While he was considering the matter, news of another troop of soldiers from towards Ft. Sill reached him.

He began to call the band of warriors to arms, but found that, through fear, many of them were slow to move, and others were advising against fighting, and cowardly hiding away. Napawat seeing this, called them squaws and upbraided them for their cowardice, but it had little effect. Fear had overcome the would-be braves. Napawat finally called out, saying,

"Seeing you are all so cowardly, and will not fight, I intend at once to go and give myself up to the soldiers, and get the best terms I can." And he turned at once and galloped away with a few followers towards army headquarters. After much difficulty and some risks, he finally reached Ft. Sill and gave himself up, promising to secure to the government all of those who continued on the warpath, if they did not surrender by a certain time.

But Tahan joined Zo-ko-yea, who went on westward, making raids wherever he could find people to murder, or plunder to steal. It was difficult to catch these marauding bands at that time, for there was such a vast unoccupied territory over which to roam, and plenty of wild game upon which to subsist. But the United States troops continued to wage war upon them with the purpose of putting down every marauding band. Most of the Indian chiefs had come in and surrendered, except Zo-ko-yea, and he had committed so many depredations that he was afraid to surrender, lest he should be killed without mercy. But he saw that he would eventually be caught, and he began to study what he should do. If he could conceal his identity and surrender, or if he could in some way prevent proof of his bloodshed and plunder, or manage to fasten it on others, he might be safe in surrendering. He felt that so far as the testimony of the Indians was concerned he was safe, for he was chief and they dare not tell anything against him. As he thought thus he glanced at Tahan, who had been with him in all his murder and plunder, and had aided him with a ruthless hand. He thought:

"Tahan is a white man. If I go in and surrender and Tahan is with me, he will be induced to tell on me. It is true he has shown himself in all our wars true to the Indian, and he knows nothing of the white man's talk and ways, but in his veins courses the white man's blood, and a like spirit that may soon spring up in friendship if he once becomes familiar with them."

The thought of this disturbed him, and while he studied about it he decided that it would never do to let Tahan be taken by the white man. It would mean death to him. The bare thought of being betrayed by Tahan angered him, although there was not the least ground for suspicion, for Tahan hated white men as bad as any Indian, and had proven it by the many bloody deeds committed upon them.

But Zo-ko-yea was in desperate mental surmisings, and the bare imagination of Tahan's betrayal haunted him. This desperate state grew more severe, till in a fit of frenzy, he whirled around and with a trembling but desperate hand drew his bow and sent an arrow whizzing through the heart of Tahan. Tahan looked with a wondering, despairing look, and without an utterance fell backwards, *dead*.

Zo-ko-yea looked upon him for awhile as he lay there upon the prairie sand, and then turned away with that last look of Tahan forever riveted upon his mind. He was left lying there to be fed upon by the wolf and the vulture; but Zo-ko-yea, savage as he was, carried the vision of his dying face upon his guilty conscience to the end of his days. He would have given the world, doubtless, could he call back the deed.

This story of Tahan's end is left in some doubt, for some of the Indians say, and Zo-ko-yea himself so claims, that after the fight with the soldiers near Llano, in their retreat across the prairie, in an almost barren region, Tahan was overcome with heat and thirst, could get no water, and that he fell by the way and died.

XVI

Indian Census Taken by Capt. R. H. Pratt.

Not long after Napawat surrendered, and was encamped with his band near Ft. Sill, Capt. R. H. Pratt was ordered by the government to take a census of the Indians. Day after day he went out to Napawat's camp to enroll the names of the Indians upon the census book. As each name was called, the Indian had to appear for himself, and answer such questions through the interpreter as were asked him. Finally, Andele was called, and as soon as Capt. Pratt saw him, he, with the other soldiers, gathered around him, for they saw that he was a captive Mexican. Andele became alarmed, and also very much angered, when they came around him and began to scrutinize him so closely. They were talking very earnestly about him, but he could not understand a word they were saying, and if there were any Indians present who did understand, they did not care for Andele to know, but they rather added to his aversion to the white man by telling him such things as would alarm his fears. As soon as they quit noticing him and left him alone, he drew up over his head and close around his face his buffalo robe so that he might not be seen so easily, and afterwards kept as much as possible out of sight of the soldiers.

However, sometime after this, Agent Tatum, hearing of a young Mexican captive among the Kiowas, sent for him. Mr. Tatum had already recovered fourteen white and twelve Mexican captives from the Indians, and he hoped to be able to identify this one and return him to his people. Andele was brought into Mr. Tatum's office, all the while in much dread, as Napawat was going with him to the office. To his surprise, however, the white agent got up from his seat and with a smiling, kindly face, met him as he went into the office and shook hands with him. He was surprised at this, and he could not understand it; for he could not understand a word that the agent was saying, but he could see the spirit of friendship in him, and his fears largely passed away. Agent Tatum tried to find out where he was captured, and about his people, but he could get no clue to his origin. The Kiowas could only tell that they bought him from the Apaches. Andele had some recollection of home and loved ones, but he dare not tell.

Mr. Tatum, hoping still to do something for Andele, asked Napawat to let Andele go to school. Napawat objected. The agent then asked that Andele be allowed to remain in his office, but still Napawat objected. And so he went back to camp.

Tatum, however, continued his efforts to get Andele, when, one day, Napawat said, "Now you and I are good friends and I don't like to refuse your request, and I will let Andele decide for himself. If he wishes to come and stay in your office, or go to school, I will agree to it; but I will let him decide it."

Mr. Tatum told Napawat that was good, and directed him to get Andele and bring him to the office. Napawat put on the air of honesty in the matter, but before taking Andele to the office, he gave him full instructions how to answer the agent, and used both honeyed words and threats lest he should answer otherwise than he directed.

Of course, therefore, when Agent Tatum made his proposition to Andele it was answered by a flat and positive refusal. And that, according to agreement, settled the matter.

XVII

Startling Incidents.
Rescue of Captives.

Before passing on, it will be of interest to relate a series of events in this connection which took place from 1869 to 1873. Under President Grant's peace policy, Lawrie Tatum, a Friend, was appointed agent for the Kiowas, Comanches and Apaches, and on July 1, 1869, undertook the duties of that office, with agency headquarters near Ft. Sill.

At that time there was one band of Comanches, the Quo-ja-les, who wandered westward towards the Rocky Mountains, living on buffalo and other wild game, and who refused to report at the agency at all. In frequent raids they stole horses from Texas, and traded them to illicit traders in New Mexico for arms and ammunition. They ridiculed the other Indians for submission to the white man, and, continuing their marauding expeditions, they formed a nucleus for other Indians who were warlike and restless under the white man's rule. They sent Agent Tatum word that they would never come to the agency and shake hands till the soldiers came out to fight them, and then, if they were whipped, they would come.

They thus set at defiance all authority till the fall of 1872, when General McKenzie, following them on one of their raids in Texas, surprised them and took one hundred of their women and children and carried them away prisoners. Soon after, the Quo-ja-les reported at the agency, acknowledged their defeat, expressed their readiness to submit, and asked that their women and children be returned to them.

"But," said Agent Tatum, "you must first bring all the white and Mexican captives you have in your band."

Perry-o-Cum, the Quo-ja-les chief, did not expect such a demand, and stood in stolid silence for some minutes, but seeing the determined look in Tatum's face, he gave instruction to his band to bring in the captives.

In a little while they brought in Adolph Kon and Clinton Smith, two Texas boys, and two others who had forgotten their names and every word of English. They remembered some of the incidents of their capture, and taking these as a clue, Agent Tatum advertised in the Texas and Kansas papers, and at last found their parents. Their names proved to be Temple Friend and Valentine Maxie. Twelve captive Mexicans were also thus rescued, and one case, that of little Presleano, was of special interest.

There was the air of superiority about him. He was bright, talkative, quick to apprehend, and sprightly in movement. He seemed to have been a pet in the home and heart of old Perry-o-Cum, the chief, and the boy loved the chief. Perry-o-Cum knew that, and felt sure that if it was left to the choice of the boy he would not be forced to give him up. So Perry-o-Cum spoke up thus:

"Agent Tatum, I am willing to give up all these other prisoners. It is right that I should, and you have a right to demand it; for they belong to your nation. But this boy is a Mexican, captured in Mexico, and he does not belong to your government, and you have no special right to him. I love him as my own son, and he loves me. I can not part from him, and I know he wants to remain with me. If you will not force him away, but leave it to his own choice, I shall be satisfied."

Tatum watched the intense anxiety of Perry-o-Cum as he spoke, and waited a little while before he replied. At last he said:

"Perry-o-Cum, what you say is good as to giving the boy his choice, and if you will let him remain here till the afternoon, we will find out what is his choice." This was readily agreed to, and the chief went away, leaving the boy in the agent's office.

Lawrie Tatum, First Kiowa Agent, with group of rescued captives. Soule (?) 1872, Smithsonian Institution.

The agent had a good dinner prepared, of which the boy partook with much relish; and while he was feeling particularly comfortable from the surroundings, and the kindness shown him, the chief was summoned to the office again. A Mexican interpreter had been secured, and after petting the boy awhile, Tatum began talking to him about his father and mother, not knowing that they were dead, and that the little boy had no memory of any father and mother, save old Perry-o-Cum and his wife. So when he put the question, "Do you wish to remain with Perry-o-Cum, or do you want to go back to your own people," to the delight of Perry-o-Cum, he said he wanted to remain with him.

"But don't you want to see your brothers and sisters? Don't you want to go to them?"

The little boy dropped his eyes in thoughtfulness a moment. The memories of home began to dawn upon him, and when he looked up again, he said, slowly and with a serious look upon his face, "I want to go home."

"Then I will send you," said Agent Tatum, and as he looked across the room at Perry-o-Cum, he saw the tears chasing each other down his otherwise stolid cheeks, but he was caught in his own proposition and he felt he must submit. The boy was returned to his people in Mexico, through General Auger, commander of the military post at San Antonio.

On July 10, 1870, a band of Kiowas went to the home of Gottlieb Koozer, in Texas. Mr. Koozer was not aware of the Indians' approach till he saw them in the yard, and being defenseless, he decided it was best to show a friendly spirit toward them, so he went out to meet them, and offered his hand in friendship. Two of them took hold of his hands at the same time in apparent friendship, while another, stepping a little to one side, shot him through the heart. They scalped him, and then went into the house, destroyed what they found therein: dresses, feather beds and many other things. They took Mrs. Koozer and her five children—one a young lady, one small girl, and three boys—and also a young man by the name of Martin B. Kilgore, who was about fourteen years of age, and started back to their reservation.

As soon as news of this outrage was received at Ft. Sill, Agent Tatum determined to rescue the prisoners, and find out and punish, if possible, the depredators. He announced to the Indians what he had heard, and declared that he would never issue any more government supplies to them till they brought the prisoners in. They demanded a ransom, for, two years before, they had been paid $1,500.00 each for some captives. He sent a letter to Mrs. Koozer by the hands of a trusty Indian, on the 7th of August, 1870. On the 18th of August the Indians, giving up any idea of fighting, went to the agency with their wives and children.

Whenever Indians are not expecting a fight, they take with them their wives and children everywhere they go, but when war is expected, they send them all away together in care of the old men. When, therefore, women and children are in sight there is assurance of peace.

They had two of the Koozer family, Miss Koozer and her little sister, with them. The little one, who had not seen her mother for several days, began crying, but was forced to hush. Indians do not allow their captives to cry. The soldiers became indignant, and stepped forward to take the captives; but in an instant the Indians pointed a dagger at the heart of the girls. The soldiers did not proceed further, for it meant sure and instant death to the girls. The Indians took them away, but seeing they could not change Agent Tatum from his purpose to withhold all government supplies till the prisoners were delivered, by 11 o'clock the two girls and two boys were brought in and delivered to him. A Mexican Kiowa had the mother, and he was stubborn and insisted upon a ransom—"a mule and a carbine."

Having delivered the above four, the Indians called for the supplies, but were informed that all of the prisoners must be brought in first. Very soon Mrs. Koozer and the other boy were brought in; but they had left young Kilgore at their camp out many miles upon the reservation. Agent Tatum then paid the Indians $100.00 apiece for the captives, lest in the future they should kill all they found on their marauding expeditions instead of taking them captive. He then issued them the usual government supplies, with the understanding that he would issue no more till M. B. Kilgore was delivered to him.

The Koozer family were a pitiable sight. Nobody can describe what Mrs. Koozer and her daughter suffered, till they found some protection and relief from an Indian woman who seemed to have more than the usual influence of a woman among the Indians. Mrs. Koozer was appropriated by a Mexican Kiowa as his wife, and he was very cruel to her, trying twice to kill her, but she was each time protected by the chiefs.

Three days later Colonel Grierson sent a detachment of soldiers to conduct Mrs. Koozer and her children to Montague, Texas, from which place she reached her home in safety. After the awful scenes of the past month and a half, what a home!

These were the last captives for whom any ransom was ever paid. Soon after this, another trial was made to extort a ransom for prisoners that utterly failed. It was about the time of the arrest of old Satanta and others. Old White Horse and six other Kiowa men and one woman went to Texas, murdered Mr. Lee and his wife and took captive their three children, Susan, aged sixteen; Millie, aged nine, and John, aged six. As soon as it was known at Ft. Sill, Agent Tatum suspended all government issues to the Indians until the captives should be brought in.

This was delayed by a proposed council, in which delegates from the civilized tribes were to be present. These civilized tribes hoped by their delegates to persuade the wild tribes to quit raiding and be peaceable. The council was set for July 22, 1872, at old Ft. Cobb, but the Kiowas did not go there till ten days after.

White Horse was stubborn, and declared that he did not want peace, but said that he and his young men would raid when and where they pleased. Lone Wolf said they would return prisoners in their possession when Satanta and Big Tree were returned from the penitentiary, all the military posts removed from the reservation, and their reservation extended from the Rio Grande to the Missouri River.

The delegates of the civilized tribes and Kicking Bird tried to pacify White Horse and Lone Wolf and other warlike Indians, but they could do but little. Agent Tatum adhered to his purpose to issue no more rations till the Lee children were brought in, and about a month later they delivered the two girls to Agent Richards at the Wichita Agency, and they were sent under care of "Caddo George," a trusty Caddo, to Agent Tatum at Ft. Sill. The boy was brought in two weeks later, and on the same day an older brother arrived from Texas and took them home.

These were the last captives the Kiowas ever took. It had become unprofitable and exceedingly dangerous, for, as Texas became more thickly settled, the people determined to put a stop to Indian raids, and they were ready to exterminate the warlike tribes, if necessary, to accomplish that end. The government, too, was proceeding by legal process to punish those who were guilty.

Reference was made above to Satanta and Big Bow's imprisonment in the penitentiary. On May 23, 1871, General Sherman called at Agent Tatum's office, and inquired if Tatum knew of any Indian band having gone to Texas recently. He said a party of Indians, about one hundred and fifty in number, had attacked a wagon train of ten wagons, seventeen miles from Ft. Richardson, killing train-master and six teamsters. Five escaped. He gave orders for McKenzie, with all the available troops at Ft. Richardson, to follow them with thirty days' rations, but as yet he had heard nothing from the pursuit.

Tatum knew nothing, but said that he thought he could find out in a few days. Four days later the Indians came to the agency for rations, and Agent Tatum invited the chiefs into his office. He told them of the tragedy reported to him by General Sherman, and asked if they knew anything about it; that he relied upon them for the truth, and was sure that they would tell him. Satanta, after a moment's silence, arose, and in the spirit of arrogance and fiendish hate, thus addressed the agent:

"Yes, I led that raid. I have been told that you have stolen a large amount of our annuity goods and given them to the Texans. I have repeatedly asked for arms and ammunition which have not been furnished, and made other requests which have not been granted. You do not listen to my talk. The white people are preparing to build a railroad through our country, which will not be permitted. Some years ago we were taken by our locks and forcibly pulled here close to Texas, where we have to fight the Texas man. Some years ago, you remember, General Custer ordered me arrested and placed in prison for several days. The memory of that outrage rankles in my soul till now, and will till the last white man goes down and rots into the dust again. Understand this, that no more Kiowas are ever to be arrested. On account of these grievances, a short time ago, I took about one hundred of my young warriors, whom I wished to train to fight, to Texas, with the chiefs, Satank, Eagle Heart, Big Tree, Big Bow and Fast Bear. We found a mule train which we captured. We killed seven of the men, and three of my men were killed, but I am willing to call it even, and it is not necessary to say anything further about it except to say that we do not expect to do any more raiding this summer, but I want you to understand that I led that Texas raid, and if anyone else claims the honor of it, he will be lying, for I am the man."

He sat down, and Satank, Big Tree, and Eagle Heart, who were present, confirmed the statement. As soon as Agent Tatum could get away, he left his office, hurried to the fort and requested Col. Grierson to arrest the six chiefs who had been participants in that raid.

Scarcely had the order been given, when Satanta took the fort interpreter and proceeded to Col. Grierson's office. He had heard that a big Washington chief (General Sherman) was there, and he wanted to see how he measured up with him. He was promptly arrested. Col. Grierson sent for Satank and Eagle Heart. Satank reached the office, and was also arrested, and Big Tree was found just outside, and while he was being arrested Eagle Heart took the alarm and fled. Kicking Bird, who had for a long time been friendly and

Vittoriano, a Mexican-Kiowa Captive.
Soule (?) 1872, Smithsonian Institution.

peaceable, plead for the release of the prisoners; but here was the opportunity of impressing a great lesson upon the Indians, and they must learn it.

A few days after these arrests, Col. McKenzie arrived from Ft. Richardson. Heavy rains had obliterated the tracks of the raiders so they could not be followed, so he had pressed on to Ft. Sill, believing that the marauding band came from the Kiowa tribe. The prisoners were placed in his charge, and in a few days he started with them to

Texas for trial. Satank was so refractory that he was put into a wagon with two soldiers, and Satanta and Big Tree into another. They were all heavily manacled. George Washington, a Caddo Indian, rode on horseback along by the wagon. This was May 28, 1871.

"My friend," said Satank to George, "I wish to send by you a little message to my people. Tell them that I am dead, I died the first day out, and my bones will be lying on the roadside. I wish my people to gather them up and take them home."

Satanta also sent a message: "Tell my people to take forty-one mules that we stole from Texas to the agent, as he and Col. Grierson requires. Don't commit any more depredations around Ft. Sill or in Texas."

In a little while Satank began to sing his death song. He was still in sight of the post—scarcely a mile away. With his back to the guards, he slipped the shackles from his wrists by taking the skin with them. He seized a butcherknife that in some mysterious way had been concealed upon his person, and started for the guards in the front part of the wagon. He struck at one of them, but missing his body made a slight wound in his leg. Both of the guards jumped from the wagon leaving their guns. Fortunately the guns were not loaded.

Satank seized one and began loading, declaring it would be sweet to die, if only he could kill one more "pale face." But, as he was pushing in the cartridge to its place, several shots from the other guards put an end to Satank's efforts. He fell from the wagon, and in about twenty minutes died in great agony, gritting his teeth in defiance to the end. By order of Col. Grierson his body was buried at Ft. Sill; but he gave the Indians the privilege of taking it up and burying it elsewhere if they chose; but they never moved it.

Satanta and Big Tree were taken on to Jacksboro, Texas, and tried for murder. Satanta was found guilty and sentenced to be hung, but his sentence was commuted to life imprisonment. He entered the Texas penitentiary, November 2, 1871. Upon recommendation of President Grant, Governor Davis, of Texas, let Satanta out, August 9, 1873, upon parole, conditioned upon good behavior. He violated his parole and was re-arrested by General Sheridan and sent back to the penitentiary, November 8, 1873. After five years of a reticent stoical life in the penitentiary, he committed suicide, Oct. 11, 1878, by jumping out of the second story window of the prison hospital.

~

XVIII

Andele is Disgusted with Indian Medicine.

The events related in the last few chapters made a profound impression upon Andele, and had a tendency to change the whole current of his thoughts and purposes. Could he have understood the white man's tongue and known the effort that the agent had made to get him out of the clutches of the Indians and the Indian ways, his life for the next few years following would have been quite different. As it was, for some time he kept as much as possible out of sight of the agent and the soldiers, lest he should be taken by force from the Indians and carried, he knew not where. The Indians had so impressed him that he feared the whites, and he thought it was safe to stay away from them.

These scenes of sickening carnage and defeat had knocked the "buffalo medicine" out of his purpose entirely, and he determined to follow more peaceful pursuits. He began to turn his attention more particularly to the course of Indian medicine for the sick, but he was doomed very soon to disappointment and disgust in this also, for, in the early part of 1873, Napawat fell sick, and, in spite of all the superstitious performances of the medicine men, died. Onkoite, his brother, succeeded him and took up Napawat's "medicine."

By permission of the government, he made two big dances in their superstitious worship, but he also fell sick. Andele did all he could himself, but felt that he was too young in the cause to trust his own skill in exorcising the evil spirits of disease, or applying whatever real remedies that Indians had any knowledge of. Indians have some real remedies, but the difficulty with them is, that if they hit upon some remedy that is good in one disease, they conclude that it is good in all diseases, and apply it accordingly. The reason of this is, that they believe there is a spirit in the medicine, and if that spirit is friendly to them in one case, it will be in all cases. And this is also the reason they sing and worship and go through a wild, weird performance while applying any real medicine. Whether they apply a real remedy, or merely go through with a performance, they call it all "making medicine." Sometimes they "make medicine" to bring rain or bring about some other desired thing.

Andele was anxious to get Onkoite cured. So he went for the best medicine men in the nation. He first got To-no-kup, a tall eagle-eyed old Indian, who was famed among his people as a physician. There are certain things that the medicine-man demands for his services and that must be given in order to make the medicine effective. In addition to these things, other things are to be given at the discretion of the patient's family or friends. In this case To-no-kup demanded a horse and some eagle feathers. Andele promised these things in behalf of Onkoite, and then also promised four other things of value.

After everything was complete, the medicine-man approached the sick man's tepee, and after some incantations at the door, he entered. He sat down, lit his pipe, and smoked, offering the smoke as he puffed it from his mouth in prayer to the sun. He then began to apply suction with his mouth to the throat and chest of the patient and spitting out before all the accumulations gathered in his mouth.

Finally, with much affectation, he spat out a small fish with a vessel of water. He declared that now the patient would be all right, for the cause of his suffering was now taken out. He took his pony, eagle feathers, and other things and went away.

Onkoite continued to grow worse. Andele went for Pho-do-dle, who came, after assurance of ample remuneration, and going through the usual ceremony of smoking and worship to the sun, he applied suction to the throat, chest and abdomen of the sufferer, and finally spat out upon the floor of the tepee a small but living snake. He looked on with affected horror, then killed the snake and buried it near the center of the tepee. The case is surely cured now, so declared the medicine-man, and so thought Andele. Pho-do-dle took his fee and left.

But to Andele's surprise, Onkoite still grew worse, and next he went for Zon-ko, or Ee-e-pan, a man of much note, whose medicine was supposed to be good. Zon-ko came, demanding the same assurance from Andele of a good fee, and after a similar worship with the others he also applied suction in the name of his special god, to the man's throat and chest and abdomen, and at last spat out a small turtle.

"These other doctors," said Zon-ko, "were lying, and their medicine was no good, but Onkoite will now get well quick; for how could a man get well with such a creature as that in him?"

Andele was sure now that the disease was cured, and very soon Onkoite would get up, and he wished as he looked at Zon-ko, that he had his skill for healing the sick. He hoped to have some day. So he paid Zon-ko, and the old man marched away as really self-deluded as he had deluded others. While he knew he had put the young turtle into his mouth himself, yet he felt that he had fallen upon the very expedient that his god could use.

But Onkoite grew worse now very fast. Andele hurried out across the prairie to old Womte's tepee.

"Womte," said he, after he had smoke a little while, "you must come quick, Onkoite is about to die. I have had three doctors to see him, and I thought in each case he was cured, but since the last one left him he has grown worse very fast. Come quick, Womte, and I will give you whatever you ask. I want you to make your medicine strong."

"My medicine is good," said Womte, "and I will cure him; I'll come soon."

Andele left Womte and returned to Onkoite. He was failing fast. Womte came with usual ceremony and went through the form of worship, and as the others had done, he also applied suction, and at last, with a grunt of apparent satisfaction, but only to call notice, he spat out upon the ground a lizard.

He killed the reptile and buried it in the center of the tepee, then declaring the medicine good, and the patient out of further danger, he arose, took his fee, and walked away. In a few minutes Onkoite fell back upon his buffalo robe and breathed no more. Womte heard the howling of the squaws and knew that his medicine was a fraud, but little did he care as long as his practice brought him ponies and eagle feathers and robes.

Andele looked on in blank astonishment, but said not a word. A complete revolution had taken place in just a few minutes in his convictions as to the Indian "Medicine Chiefs." He had forever lost confidence in them, and as soon as he met one of them he declared with spirit, "I have no confidence in your medicine; I'll never make another offering, nor pay another thing to one of you. I did want your shield and to learn your ways, but I want it no longer. Four of you waited on Onkoite, and you see he is dead. Each one of you declared he was cured, but you see he is *dead*. I have no more faith in my dreams nor in your medicine."

As he closed this speech he turned away. It would have been a dangerous speech that would have brought down the maledictions of the whole tribe had not Onkoite's case been fresh in their minds. As it was, the convictions of the crowd who were listening were with him. This event had much to do with preparing Andele for seeking a better way.

XIX

Andele Marries—Has Trouble

There are three ways of obtaining a wife among the Indians. First, a young man often steals his wife. He will get his own sister to talk to the girl for him, and let her know his heart, and if she reciprocates, a clandestine meeting is arranged, and the two go off together, and sometimes can not be found for a long while. As soon as the parents of the girl find out who has their daughter, they go to the home of the young man's father and proceed to take everything they can find belonging to the family: robes, blankets, provisions, and even the tepee itself. This becomes a frolic enjoyed by everyone, except the family being robbed. Nobody interferes or objects to the robbing, unless the daughter who has eloped was of doubtful character. In that case, no price is expected for her, and none is allowed. Stumbling Bear came to the writer's house once, deposited a lot of goods and left them a long time. One day when he was in, thinking he had forgotten about them, his attention was called to them, when he said in his good-humored way, "Me savey. Me no take 'em now. May be so pretty soon me boy catch 'em squaw. Indian all come me

camp, heap steal 'em. Stay here, no find 'em. Me come catch em,"
and like a prudent man he foresaw the evil and provided against it.

The second way of getting a wife is more civil. A young man falls
in love with a young woman. Often he will take his flute, and in
stilly eve go somewhere near her father's tepee, and pour forth his
heart yearnings in music, consisting of about two notes. It is a monotonous sound, but often it is the sweetest music to the girl as she
listens. To woo or be wooed is fascinating, and often a response to
this particular method results in a clandestine meeting and elope-
ment as above described in the first case.

The third way is a straight out trade. The man sees a woman
whom he would like to make his wife. He goes to the girl's parents
and proposes a trade—so many ponies or blankets or buffalo robes
for the girl. If it is agreeable, the trade is made, and the girl is given
over to the man as soon as the property is delivered. The girl, in
most cases, has no choice in the matter, and is not consulted. Sometimes, ten or twelve year old girls are thus traded off to an old man
who perhaps has several wives already.

Andele had now grown up and become a mature young man, and
companionship naturally became the wish of his heart. He had been
with eager eyes, watching the movements of Tonko, old Keabi's
daughter, and felt somewhat the movings of the heart that perhaps
Samson felt when looked upon the daughter of the Philistine, and
she was destined to prove somewhat of a Delilah to him, as we shall
soon see. Without speaking to her about the matter at all, he went
one day to old Keabi and proposed a trade for his daughter.

"What will you give me?" said Keabi.

"Whatever you ask," replied Andele.

"Give me one good pony and two buffalo robes," said Keabi. The
trade was closed, and Tonko went to be Andele's wife.

But the arrangement was not a happy one, and very soon signs of
unfaithfulness were seen in Tonko, and one day while Andele was
gone, Tonko eloped with Ton-kea-mo-tle. Andele did not care,—was
rather glad to get rid of her so easily. She did not suit him, and she
was dissatisfied with him. He did not even go to ask her to come
back, and thus the matter would have ended; but Af-poo-dle, his
Indian brother, thought this was so out of the Indian way, that he
upbraided Andele with cowardice in not demanding satisfaction of
Ton-kea-mo-tle, as was his right.

"Af-poo-dle, since you brand me as a coward, you get ready for trouble, for you know, in a case of this kind, a brother must stand with a brother, and if I have war with Ton-kea-mo-tle, it becomes your war as well. You may get ready, for I will call Ton-kea-mo-tle to account, and we shall have trouble."

"All right," replied Af-poo-dle. "I am not afraid. I will stand by you. My sleep would not be sweet, if I deserted you in the time of war."

At once Andele mounted his pony and went galloping across the prairie toward a cluster of tepees nestling close in the edge of a little skirt of mesquite saplings about five miles in the distance. Reaching the encampment he asked for Ton-kea-mo-tle.

"He is gone away to Ft. Sill, and will come at the setting of the sun," said an old squaw, who sat near the entrance of the tepee. Andele rode away disappointed, but next morning he went again to Ton-kea-mo-tle's tepee, but was told that he had gone to another village in the distance. He rode away again, and returned again, and again Ton-kea-mo-tle had gone away.

"I'll make him see me," said Andele to himself, as he rode out upon the prairie towards a herd of ponies belonging to Ton-kea-mo-tle. In the herd was a very fine pony, Ton-kea-mo-tle's pet and best rider. He raised his six shooter and with steady aim fired. The horse fell dead, pierced through the heart. He then killed two others and rode away. "Af-poo-dle, my brother," he said, as he reached his camp again and dismounted, "you may get ready, for I could not get Ton-kea-mo-tle to meet me, and three of his best horses are lying out upon the prairie yonder, ready for the coyotes or his squaws."

"Umph?" grunted Af-pood-dle in approval, but at the same time he looked as if he had rather there was some other way of settling difficulties than this Indian way. He prepared for trouble, however; for he knew a deadly conflict was brewing, and he knew not where it would end.

In a few days there was a large gathering of Indians on Cache Creek. The brothers of Ton-kea-mo-tle urged him to take advantage of that occasion to surprise Andele and kill him without warning, but Andele knew the Indian character too well to be off guard, so he and Af-poo-dle watched closely every movement of Ton-kea-mo-tle and his friends. It was near the middle of the day, when someone warned Af-poo-dle of Ton-kea-mo-tle's movements and purpose. He had arranged to go off across the prairie, as though leaving for his camp some miles away, but to return from another direction and come upon Andele unexpectedly from a little cañon near by. Learning this, Andele and Af-poo-dle slipped unnoticed into the entrance of the cañon, so that they would have a commanding view of its full length.

They had but a short while to wait, for they heard voices not far away, and upon nearer approach, Andele heard Ton-kea-mo-tle saying, "We will kill him; he is nothing but a Mexican, a captive, and yet he tries to act as if he were a Kiowa, and had the rights and privileges of a Kiowa."

Andele grasped his rifle more firmly, for in some way the whole crowd had on some marauding expedition secured rifles and ammunition.

"Be ready and firm and brave now, Af-poo-dle, for the time is come, and we must prove ourselves worthy of a good wife. As for myself, I am ready to die, but I will die like a man, and I will get Ton-kea-mo-tle before I go. Ready, quietly," said Andele.

Just at the moment, Ton-kea-mo-tle reached the edge of the cañon, and was in the act of descending the slope, when he discovered Andele, and Af-poo-dle close beside him. He raised his rifle, but before he could get it to his shoulders, Andele fired. It was so quick and unexpected that Ton-kea-mo-tle and his comrades rolled over an embankment and disappeared. Nobody was hurt, for Andele had missed his mark, but his enemy was so panic stricken at his narrow escape that he did not return to the conflict.

The whole encampment, however, rushed out to see what was the trouble, and demand an explanation, but when it was learned that Andele had been wronged by Ton-kea-mo-tle decoying his wife away from him, he was fully exonerated for shooting at Ton-kea-mo-tle and also for killing his horses.

This settled the difficulty for that day, but it created a breach that could not be healed so soon. Three years after this occurrence, Andele was riding along one day alone, out of sight of all habitations, and entering a narrow passage way around the mountain side, he discovered his old enemy, Ton-kea-mo-tle, approaching.

"Now our trouble will be settled, for here one of us will die. There is no way to avoid meeting, and this means a deadly conflict," said Andele to himself, and he felt for his arms, but discovered to his consternation that he had failed to arm himself when leaving his camp.

He dared not turn his back upon his enemy; he was too proud for that, and besides there was more danger in running in this instance than going boldly forward. He resorted to strategy. He placed his hands as in position for grasping a six shooter, quickened his pace forward, and watched with intense gaze his enemy's movements. He was prepared for the worst, but as Ton-kea-mo-tle approached, he called out:

"Andele, my friend, we have been enemies a long time and I am tired of it. If you are willing, let us drop our difficulty and be friends."

"Ka-tai-ke" (good), replied Andele, but too glad of the opportunity to settle the matter. From the first he had not cared to have any difficulty, but according to Indian custom he could not do otherwise and be respected by the people. The pressure of public sentiment forces to many a foolish act, even among the civilized.

He had now vindicated his claim to courage and exonerated himself from the charge of cowardice, and he did not care to push the matter further. And hence he made friends with Ton-kea-mo-tle, and did not mete out any punishment to his wicked wife. When he was first brought home by the Kiowas years ago, he saw old Big Bow cut off his wife's nose and tie it around a boy's neck.

This was the punishment usually inflicted upon a wife for infidelity to her husband, and often several fingers were also cut off, and sometimes the woman was killed. Asha, an old Comanche chief, had a wife to elope with a young man who was nearer her own age. Asha, with a few friends, sought for her many moons, but in vain, till one day, taking a special friend, he started westward to visit the Navajoes. After many days he reached a Navajo settlement, and riding up to a tepee, to his surprise and gratification, he found the young Comanche who had eloped with his wife.

"Where is my wife?" he asked. Without speaking a word, the young man pointed to the tepee. Asha entered.

For some while neither spoke, but at last, in words of mock affection, Asha gave vent to the fiendish feelings in his soul. Without meting out any vengeance upon the young man, he took, as if often done in such cases, such property belonging to him as he could utilize. Taking his wife, he and his friend started for home at once; for he was anxious to get where he would feel free to vent his vengeance upon the woman who had been so untrue to him. One evening, as the sun went down, the three crossed the Red River into the Comanche country. They had traveled many days and were worn with fatigue. But now they were on their own territory and felt rested. They camped for the night. Next morning, after the woman had prepared the breakfast of jerked buffalo and fat, and the two men had eaten and smoked their cigarettes, made of dried sumac leaves, and the woman had caught the horses and packed everything ready for travel, old Asha called the woman before him. He began:

"You are a bad squaw, fit only for the coyotes. We are now back in our own country. I will give you the choice between two things: Have your nose cut off, or be killed."

The woman stood there in the yellow sunlight of that October morning, a pitiable object, but showing not the least sign of emotion. She waited for sometime, but at last with steady voice spoke:

"If I go back among my people with my nose cut off, and my face disfigured, I shall always be the object of scorn and ridicule. I can never expect anything but cruelty at the hands of him who bought me of my father for a dozen ponies and a few buffalo hides, and although old enough to be my grandfather, forced me, contrary to my cries, to be his wife. Besides, my heart is back yonder with the young man in the Navajoe camp, and I would prefer death without him, to life with you. You can kill me. Let it be quick."

So brave and true was this speech, that Asha hesitated, but as he had given her the choice, he was, according to Indian custom, bound to comply. He turned to his friend and requested him to shoot her.

"No," said the friend, "she is your wife. I have no grievance against her. Shoot her yourself."

Asha turned to his wife. Somehow, in this extreme hour, she had grown confident, and something of the light of her girlhood had returned to her face, and she stood there, her searching eyes looking large upon Asha. He again hesitated, for her mute gaze spoke louder than she could speak in words. But he had given her her choice. She chose death, and it could not be reversed, unless she asked it. She would not ask it.

"Quit looking at me," said Asha, "I can not shoot you while your eyes are upon me; turn your back."

What an influence to deter, or to encourage, there is in the human gaze at times. She promptly turned her back, and in an instant the bow string tightened and relaxed, and the arrow went whizzing through the woman's heart. The men hurriedly mounted their horses and rode away, leaving the body to be eaten by coyotes. Such is the Indian custom.

As among all heathen people, marriage among the Kiowas is held very loosely. Andele, in a short time, married another woman, but in a little while put her away, having found no congeniality on account of disparity in age, she being rather an old woman.

It is often the case that the chiefs take the younger and better-looking women and leave none for the young men except old squaws, and thus it is not infrequent that a young man may be seen leading around a woman old enough for his mother.

About one year after this, he fell in love with a pretty young Indian woman, *Ti-it-ti,* or "White Sage." She was tender in her attention to him, and faithful in her affections, and they lived happily together till her death.

One of the singular customs of the Indians is that a son-in-law and mother-in-law are not allowed to speak directly to each other, but must communicate with each other through the wife and daughter. If it becomes absolutely necessary to ask a question, and the wife is not present, the son-in-law can turn away his head, and looking in another direction, ask the question. The mother-in-law can answer in the way. A sister-in-law must be dealt with in the same way. A son-in-law may, by special favors to his father-in-law, claim the next younger daughter, and by continued favors, still the next, and on till he has every daughter in the family. Even a boy receiving special favors from a man may, to show his gratitude, give away his sister, and the family will feel bound by the arrangement. Often a man will pet a boy, bestow presents upon him, gain his favor, and then ask him for his sister.

At this date there is a twelve-year old boy, Ernest Kickingbird, in Methvin Institute, who has a young sister. Recently an old Indian visited the school, petted Ernest, and asked him for his sister. Ernest agreed to it, but when the man went to Kickingbird himself, and claimed the girl, he was flatly refused. Kickingbird had learned too much of a better way himself to allow his daughter to be sacrificed at the mere whim or choice of her brother.

XX

Dog Soldiers

It will be of interest here to give an account of the Kiowa Indian soldiery.

Every child, both male and female, is born a *Pho-li-yo-ye*, or rabbit. From the very beginning they are taken into "the circle" and initiated; and as soon as they first begin to totter on their little feet they are taught to dance in the circle of "rabbits." An old man is put in charge of the "rabbits," and when a big feast and dance is to be held, the old man goes throughout the camps calling out: "Rabbits, rabbits, get ready; paint your faces; be prompt; come to the dance; plenty to eat—grand time!"

And very soon, from every direction, they come together at the place designated, boys and girls of all sizes and ages, from the least to those just blooming into manhood and womanhood. They dance, or rather jump around in a circle, mimicing, as much as possible, the motion of a rabbit, and keeping time with the two forefingers of each hand, lifted like rabbits' feet in running, and at the same time, making a slight noise like the rabbit. The only music accompanying the performance is the tom-tom. Thus the young people are brought up and kept organized for the more trying life of a soldier; for every boy, as soon as old enough, becomes a soldier, and of course, every girl must needs become a soldier's wife.

There are five orders of soldiers. The *Ti-e-pa-ko*, the *Tsai-e-ton-mo*, the *Ton-kon-ko*, the *Ah-tle-to-yo-ye*, and the *Ko-e-Tsain-ko*. The five orders make up the whole army of "Dog Soldiers." The last-mentioned band is composed exclusively of those who have distinguished themselves in war. Any number of the other orders may become a Ko-e-Tsain-ko who has achieved some notable deed. They are distinguished in dress by a red sash made of painted skins, and they use only the deer hoof rattle in all their religious performances, instead of the usual rattle-gourd.

These different orders of soldiers are constantly watching the "rabbits" as they grow up, and as soon as one of them is old enough to catch for the army, it is a race between the different orders to catch him and add him to their ranks. By this means the ranks of the Dog Soldiers are kept filled by captives from the "rabbits."

When a "rabbit" is captured by one of the orders he is sent to capture another "rabbit," who is to be his file man and close companion in the army. The Ah-tle-to-yo-ye captured Gno-ah-tone.

"Now go," said the chief, "and select another 'rabbit' to be your comrade in the order."

Gno-ah-tone went at once while it was not yet light in search of Andele. He found him lying asleep in his wigwam. Gno-ah-tone sat down beside him and awoke him.

"Andele, you and I have grown to manhood now, and can no longer remain among the 'rabbits.' The time has come for us to join the ranks of the braves, who go to war for scalps and plunder. The Ah-tle-to-yo-ye have put their hands upon me and sent me to select another 'rabbit' for companion in their ranks. I come in the early morning to claim you for that service and make you my friend and companion forever."

While he was talking he was at the same time preparing the deer bone pipe for use, and lighting it, he drew a few whiffs and puffed the smoke upward to the sun, praying as he did so. Turning then to Andele he gave him the pipe, who did as Gno-ah-tone had done, and thus he became an Ah-tle-to-yo-ye, as boon companion to Gno-ah-tone, henceforth ready to sacrifice their lives one for the other.

It is a curious use the Indian makes of the pipe. Usually when smoking for pleasure, they use only the cigarette made of a mixture of sumac leaves and tobacco, enclosed in a green leaf covering, plucked from a shrub or tree near by. But they use pipes in worship, or when a pledge is to be taken or given. A man who wants to go on the warpath to avenge the blood of a friend or relative, calls his friends together, or whomsoever he wishes to join him, and after making known his business he lights his pipe, smokes a few whiffs, and prays as he puffs the smoke towards the sun, and then passes it to the next, and on to the next, till all have had an opportunity to smoke. One may decline to smoke without any insult, and will be exempt from going on the warpath, but if he smokes he dare not fail or refuse to go lest some great evil befall him. Thus by smoking the pipe, he pledges himself to whatever is proposed on that occasion.

XXI

Light Dawning

Andele had for years lived a veritable Indian. Yet, as the years rolled by, he saw the wretchedness of the Indian life and became disgusted with it. Nevertheless some of the Indian ways had become his fixed habit, and any effort to change them by others offended him.

But light was beginning to dawn upon him. He could see as far as he had been brought into contact with them, the strength and thrift of the white men, and he had gone at one time with an Indian wagon train two hundred miles away to Caddo, and had seen there a railroad train. It set him to thinking that there must be something better for him than wandering in blanket and wild robe over the prairies like the wild buffalo. The buffalo were fast being killed out by the restless, aggressive white man, and it was probable that the Indian would go likewise, unless there was a change; for the white man seemed as glad to kill an Indian as a buffalo.

One day he heard the United States agent, George Hunt, talking to the Indians through an interpreter. He said:

"The Great Father at Washington wants all your young men to learn how to work, so that they may make money and have homes and be peaceable."

"I'll do it," said Andrés to himself. "I will go at once and ask the agent for work. I'll change my life now."

That same day he took an interpreter to the agent and explained what he wanted, and asked for work. He was put into the government blacksmith shop to learn that trade. He was a wild looking spectacle, and awkward enough in a blacksmith shop with all his Indian paraphernalia on, full rigged and ornamented. But he was honest and earnest in his purpose to learn, and soon began to show progress.

New things were constantly opening to him as he was brought more directly in contact with the whites, when one day he happened to be in the store of an Indian trader where a post office had been established. He had seen people trading with the merchants, receiving goods over the counter for which they paid money, but he noticed now the merchant seemed to be handing out things for which the people paid nothing. He could not understand it, and his curiosity was so much excited, that he asked the blacksmith, under whom he worked, what it meant. The blacksmith answered that the people were getting messages from their friends; that people could talk on paper to one another although they were a long distance apart. He said no more, but it awakened a hope and set him to thinking, and thus he soliloquized:

"Long years ago, I was stolen from my home. The Apaches stole me. Now, as I think of it, it all comes fresh to my memory. The Indians call me Andele, but my name is Andrés. My father, who was he?"

He sat straining his memory, going back, back, over the wild scenes of his Indian life, through the years since he was stolen by the Mescaleros in the little vega where he tended the cows.

"Who was my father?" and occasionally memory would almost catch back the long forgotten name, but then—

"Now I have it!" he exclaimed. "I remember now, it is Martínez. Martínez, Martínez; yes, that is it," and he continued to pronounce it, lest it should slip from him again.

It was night, and he went to his bed and lay down, but could not sleep. His mind was full of thoughts of home, mother, the scenes of his childhood. Memories long since dead were revived. He lay there wondering, and the more he thought, the more wide awake and restless he became. Hope began to spring up in his heart, and he arose and made his way at that late hour to the sleeping apartment of the United States physician, Dr. Hugh Tobin. He rapped at the door, when Dr. Tobin bade him come in; for although it was late, he had not yet retired.

"Why, what brings you here at this late hour, Andele? Anybody sick?" asked Dr. Tobin, in the Comanche dialect; for he and Andele both had some knowledge of that language.

"I am come," replied Andele, "to tell you something that disturbs me much, and keeps me from sleeping. I am, as you know, a Mexican captive. I learned to-day that people may communicate with their friends on paper through the post office. I have been thinking it may be possible for me to find out my people from whom I was stolen long years ago when I was a small child. Do you think I could?" and he looked anxiously and intently into Dr. Tobin's face as he asked the question.

"Do you remember the place where your father lived, and do you remember your father's name?" asked Dr. Tobin.

"I have been lying awake on my bed, thinking, thinking, oh, so hard, and at last my father's name has come to me. It is Martínez, and the place close to our home was Las Vegas, and my oldest brother was named Dionicio. I remember him well, now."

"Well," said Dr. Tobin, "we will write to your brother, because if your father was an old man at the time of your capture, he is probably dead ere this."

"Will you please write now," asked Andele, as his heart beat in ever increasing interest.

"I will," said Dr. Tobin, and he turned to his desk and penned the following brief note:

KIOWA AND COMANCHE U.S. AGENCY,
ANADARKO, IND. TER., JAN. 6, 1883.
DIONICIO MARTÍNEZ,
LAS VEGAS, N.M.

DEAR SIR: Did you have a little brother stolen by the Indians many years ago, by name Andrés? The Indians call him Andele. If so, write me at once. He is here, and we think can be identified fully. Respectfully,

HUGH TOBIN,
U.S. Physician.

"Now," said Dr. Tobin, "this letter will reach Las Vegas in about ten days, and if your brother is there, he will get it. In thirty days this letter will come back if your brother didn't get it. Be patient and we shall hear."

Andele went back to his own bed, but he could not sleep. The vague memories of the long ago came flooding his mind and heart, growing more and more distinct, till they stood before him as but the happenings of yesterday. After a month had elapsed, the letter came back, not having been called for at Las Vegas. It was a sore disappointment, for Andele felt confident that it would reach his brother. Dr. Tobin encouraged him to hope, and he wrote the second letter, but it, too, came back after some delay. But Andele seemed more determined to hear from his people, and he continued to send letters for nearly two years, till one day, Dionicio Martínez, who had years before moved with his family to Trinidad, happened to be on a visit to his mother in Las Vegas, and received Andele's letter.

He did not break the seal of the letter till he reached the house and sat down near his mother. He was so astonished when he read the letter, he could scarcely restrain an outcry; but fearing lest the news should too deeply affect his old white-haired mother, he, with a great effort, tried to conceal his emotions. The quick eye of the mother detected something unusual, and she asked:

"What is it, my son? Is there some evil news in your letter? Is someone sick? Tell me at once, for I see something is wrong."

"No, mother," said Dionicio, "no evil news, but good news. I hardly know how to tell you. Will you please nerve yourself to hear something that will surprise you much?"

"Well, tell me quick, for you hold me in suspense."

"Mother, will you be prepared to hear that our little Andrés, whom the Indians stole long years ago, is still living and here is a letter from—"

But before he could finish the sentence the white-haired mother had swooned away, and was falling from her chair. It was an affecting scene, and here we draw the curtain.

~

XXII

Goes Home to New Mexico.
Returns after Four Years.
Converted and Joins the Methodist Church.
God's Providence in It All.

After correspondence with Dr. Tobin and the United States Agent, Hon. George Hunt, at Anadarko, and Andele was thoroughly identified, Dionicio started in a hack across the country to Anadarko to take Andele home. He was several weeks on the road, but made a successful trip. When he reached the agency, and Andele was brought before him, he looked at him in open-eyed wonder. Andele was dressed in full Indian paraphernalia, hair long and plaited, and rolled in beaver skin; face painted, beaded moccasins and fringed buckskin leggings on; but in spite of all this Indian dress, Dionicio could detect the family resemblance in the features of Andele, and after closer examination, his identification was complete.

The Indians called a council, for they were decidedly opposed to giving Andele up unless it was very certain that his real brother had come for him. But after hearing a full account of his capture by the marauding Mescaleros, and knowing that it was from them they had bought him long years ago, they were satisfied and willing for him to go, but insisting that he must come back after a visit home.

In a few days he started with his brother for Las Vegas, where he arrived on the 19th day of March, 1885, having been just a month on the road.

It would hardly be proper to intrude upon the privacy of the home and undertake to describe the meeting that took place. The white-haired mother, tottering under the weight of years, under the impulse of a mother's love, knew him as he entered the door, although he still wore some of the Indian paraphernalia. She could hardly endure the excess of joy as she hugged him to her heart, and called him her own little boy.

Twenty long years of sorrowing, in slow succession had dragged their weary length along. Storm-swept and weather-beaten the old earth seemed to have grown gray, but even yet she had been spared to see her little boy. Andrés stood before her a mature man, but to her he was still the *"Mi Muchachito"* (my little boy) of the long years ago, and thus she caressed him with the same fondness and tenderness as in the days of his infancy.

Andrés remained with his people till the summer of 1889, and then, after four years, in which he completely recovered the Spanish language, his mother tongue, he returned to the Indians. His wife, "White Sage," had died during his absence, but his interests were all identified with the Kiowas, and he had learned to love them. Besides, God has a purpose in it all, for in the apparent calamity that had come to Andrés in his capture, God was overruling it all in preparing him for a life that should glorify him. We shall see as we read on.

God works in mysterious ways, and often His plans are many years in execution.

In the fall of 1887, at the session of the Indian Mission Conference, held in Vinita, Indian Territory, Bishop Galloway presiding, contrary to all expectation and to all apparent wisdom, the author was sent, "Missionary to the Wild Tribes." But satisfied that it was God's direction, and conscious of His presence, he went with a glad heart and began work among them, with headquarters at Anadarko.

Here he had toiled faithfully for two years, having built in the meantime a parsonage with a "church annex," when one day out upon his rounds among the tepees, he discovered standing on the banks of the Washita, near the old government commissary building, a Mexican whom he had not before seen. Approaching him, he said: "You are a stranger here. I have not seen you before."

"No," replied the Mexican, "I am no stranger here. I belong here, but I have been away for four years over in New Mexico."

He spoke in such broken English that it was difficult to understand him.

"Well, I am a Methodist preacher, a missionary sent here by the church, and I want to know all the people, and help them where I can. What is your name?"

"My name," he replied, "is Andrés Martínez, but the Indians call me Andele, and everybody calls me by my Indian name."

"I have a little church right up beyond the post office, and will be glad to have you come to our services tomorrow."

"I will come," said he.

The next day, Sunday, the little church was well filled with blanket Indians of the numerous tribes that inhabit both sides of the Washita, and a few Mexicans, among whom was Andele. All were attentive listeners, but Andele seemed profoundly interested. He was a constant attendant from that time on.

On Sabbath morning, at the 11 o'clock service, a call was made for all those who felt that they were sinners, and wanted right then to give themselves to the Lord, and be saved, to come to the altar. Andele, sitting in the back part of the house, arose, came forward, and knelt at the altar. Without manifesting any great emotion, he professed saving faith in Christ, and on the next Sabbath asked for church membership.

When he came forward to be received into the church on the next Sabbath, however, it was evident that there was some great conflict going on within. It was not fully understood till sometime after, he told of his childhood home, his capture by the Mescaleros, his transfer to the Kiowas, his training among them, his disappointment in the Indian religion, and after his rescue and return home, his continued disappointment in a mere ritualistic form of worship, and finally, his deep conviction as to the truth of God's word and his own sinfulness and need, as he heard the author, from time to time, read and explain the Bible; and then, amid, but in spite of, much embarrassment, lest he should be ridiculed, he determined to give himself up to God in Christ's name, and in the act realized His power to save.

I have gone over it all in this little volume as he has related it from the beginning. It is no difficult matter to trace the Lord's loving hand in it all. It is the overruling of His providence to bring good out of evil; for brought up by the stubborn and warlike Kiowas, trained in trial, inured to hardships, skilled in their ways, acquainted with their superstitions, a perfect knowledge of their language, and

Andrés Martínez (*Än'dali*) in 1894. Hillers 1894, Smithsonian Institution.

several other Indian dialects as well, and having a fair knowledge both of English and Spanish, there is no one so well qualified under sanctifying grace to lead the Indians to Christ. He is by every token called of the Lord to carry the gospel to the Indians.

A few months after his conversion and reception into the church, he took the place of interpreter and industrial teacher in the Methvin Institute near Anadarko, Oklahoma Territory, in which capacity he labored long and well. Owned of God and respected of men, he goes forward without wavering and without a vestige of superstition clinging to him to the work to which God has, by His providence, called him, and for which He has so well qualified him.

~

XXIII

A Civilized Courtship and Christian Marriage.

This chapter must close this little volume. Ti-i-ti, or "White Sage," had now been dead about five years. She had been faithful to Andele, but while he was away in New Mexico she took sick and died.

While Andele had learned the ways of civilized life and had caught the inspiration of a better hope by faith in Christ, he had also, under this new order of things, learned the magic of successful wooing after the approved manner of Christian refinement, and having actually fallen in love, went forth to a conquest difficult but pleasing to his enraptured soul. In marauding expeditions into Texas and elsewhere, he had tried the conflict of war and bloodshed, and it was exciting in the extreme, and dangerous; and now, while in this conflict with love, choking with quickened pulsations and increased heart beats, he woke to a realization of the truth of the poet's song:

> "War and love are fierce compeers;
> War sheds blood while love shed tears;
> War breaks heads while love breaks hearts;
> War has swords while love has darts."

But nothing daunted, he pushed his conquest, as we shall see, to a successful ending.

In the spring of 1893, Miss Emma McWhorter, daughter of Rev. P.T. McWhorter, of Indian Mission Conference, took the place of matron in Methvin Institute, an Indian mission school belonging to the Woman's Board of the M.E. Church, South. She was a young lady of substantial Christian character, quiet in manners and reserved, and conscientious and faithful in discharge of duty. She served her place well in the Institute. The Indian children, as well as the old Indians, all seemed to love her, and gave her their confidence.

She being matron and Andele industrial teacher, they were thrown together occasionally, each day, in looking after the children, especially when one was sick, as each had to keep up with the prescriptions and aid in the attendance upon the sick.

One day, stepping unexpectedly into the "sick room," a scene presented itself that afforded both embarrassment and amusement. A little girl, who had been too short a time in the school to understand much English, was lying upon the bed, sick with a fever after a chill, the Matron standing at the one side, the Industrial Teacher at the other. Evidently something unintelligible to the Indian girl had been said, but full of absorbing interest to the Matron and Industrial Teacher.

As I stepped in, the Industrial Teacher looked up with a start, and startled was the Matron. The live carnation coursed itself around the cheeks of the one, and the flush of confusion covered the face of the other. The diagnosis of the case before me, not of the sick child, but of the Industrial Teacher and Matron, was easy. It took no skilled physician to read the symptoms. The symptoms of heart yearnings are more difficult to conceal than that of a fever-stricken body.

I stepped on, after inquiry after the sick child, saying to myself, "Evidently Andele is not 'making medicine' now after the fashion of the Indians preparing for war and bloodshed, but

> . . . is working his magic wand
> For wooing a heart and winning a hand."

His wooings were not in vain, and his magic did not fail. On the 17th of October, 1893, the writer solemnized the rites of holy wedlock between them, and thus the Matron and Industrial Teacher went into a life-partnership and became one!

Supplement

Since the foregoing chapters were written twenty-eight years ago, many have been the changes, through the fleeting years, and Andele has grown to be an old man, but still erect and active.

All those who were concerned with his capture and his early life have passed on from the warpath here to the peaceful haunts of the "happy hunting ground" beyond, and Indian habits and customs have changed and Indian life completely transformed.

During his early captivity by the Apaches, he was traded several times to different bands of that tribe.

He suffered so many things at their hands that he became somewhat inured to their savage life, and was rendered callous to their barbarous acts.

For the purpose of testing his skill with the bow and arrow, one day a young Apache man got Andele out and stood him up against a tree with the threat that if he moved he would kill him. The sport then stood off a certain distance, adjusted his arrow to the tense bowstring and let it fly with full force which was to prove Andele's death; but he craned his body to one side and the arrow missed him and stuck into the tree. As he was adjusting another arrow to the string, the Apache's wife, who was the little lame woman mentioned in a previous chapter, rushed to Andele's rescue, and there began a contest between her and her brutal husband that meant life or death to Andele. For some minutes the doubtful conflict went on till at last the little lame woman, bruised and bleeding, took Andele away in triumph to her tepee and to present safety. It is interesting to learn that the mother of this little lame woman still lives in a home near Mescalero, N.M., and in her Andele feels a special interest.

The last Apache who bought Andele before he was traded to the Kiowas has two sons now living near Fort Sill. Their names are Che-ba-to and De-na-to, indicating Spanish origin. They came among the Comanches years ago, became identified with that tribe, and were adopted by them.

At this last sale, Andele determined to run away into the mountains and there die, as he did not expect ever to reach home again, and he could endure their cruel treatment no longer, but just at this time the Kiowas appeared upon the scene and bought him, an account of which is given in a previous chapter.

After being traded to the Kiowas, and after long days of travel, they reached the Kiowa home north of Red River, crossing the river near the present site of Quanah, Texas.

E-ton-bo was a young unmarried daughter of Heap O' Bears, sprightly and full of vivacity. As her father, Heap O' Bears, started on this marauding expedition into Texas and Mexico, E-ton-bo called to him and said, "While you are gone, catch a pretty little boy and bring him home and give him to me to be my son." So when Andele came, she took him to her heart, and was ever a real mother to him treating him with much love and tenderness. Soon after this, E-ton-bo married Zilka, and he lived with them and his adopted grandfather, Heap O' Bears, till Heap O'Bears' tragic death at the hands of the Utes. He then went to live with Napawat, the successor of Heap O' Bears.

While he had escaped the cruel treatment of the Apaches, yet Andele was doomed to witness many acts of cruelty among the Kiowas as well; for when they reached home, Zo-ko-yea (Bigbow) learned that one of his wives had been unfaithful to him while he was away on the warpath, and, as was their custom for such an offense, he cut off her nose and strung it around the neck of Af-kon, a nephew of his. Af-kon was then a small boy, but is now an old man and still living at the time of this writing.

During these exciting times, the Indians were on frequent raids into Texas or Mexico, and many were the scalps they took and the horses they stole. Andele partook largely of their warlike spirit, and was eager to go with them on these marauding expeditions, which he did on several occasions after he grew up to young manhood.

It was about this time that the three chiefs, Tsain-tan-ta (Satanta), Tsain-tank-ya (Satank) and Big Tree led a band of warriors into Texas, and attacked a wagon train belonging to the U.S. Government, and killed all the teamsters except two who escaped. When the band returned to the reservation, they boasted to Lawrie Tatum, the U.S. Agent, of what they had done.

They were soon after arrested, and were started to Texas under military escort to be tried in the Texas courts for murder.

Several years before this event, Tsain-tank-ya's son led a band of young warriors into Texas and while there was killed. His panic stricken band left his body lying where it fell, and made haste for home. Tsain-tank-ya loved his son very much, and intending to make him his successor, he had transferred to him his own name, and he himself had assumed the name of Ka-ton-ni.

When, therefore, news of his son's death reached him, he threw off the buffalo robe which he wore summer and winter (he never wore a sheet like other Indians in summer), and began mutilating his body till his whole frame was a hideous bleeding spectacle, all the time alternately wailing for his son and shouting out the warwhoop.

He kept this up for several months, wailing morning and evening, till finally, the same band of young warriors that his son had commanded, he gathered together and led into Texas to seek revenge, and to gather up his son's bones. He found the bones and gathered them up, but before leaving Texas he killed and scalped two men, so when he reached home he had two scalps hanging to his belt.

After the usual scalp dance, he built a large buffalo tepee into which he placed his son's bones. Here he kept them for years on a bed in the west side of the tepee.

Often he held a feast in this tepee, and called in his friends to enjoy the feast with his son.

Andele was called into service on these occasions, and his place was next to the bones, and his chief duty was to fill and refill the pipe as they smoked, after eating. They usually spent most of the day at these feasts smoking and recounting their exploits in war.

At last, Tsain-tank-ya secreted the bones of his son, nobody ever knew where, and went on this last raid for which he was now arrested. His tragic death is related in a previous chapter, and need not be repeated here.

Tsain-tan-ta and Big Tree were taken on to Texas, tried for murder, found guilty, and sentenced to be hung; but the sentence was commuted to life imprisonment, and later, they were paroled upon good behavior.

Tsain-tan-ta violated his parole and was sent back to prison, where, after five years, he committed suicide by jumping out of a third story window to the pavement below.

Big Tree is still living at this writing, a quiet, peaceable old man, a consistent member of the Baptist church.

Andele was a witness to all these exciting scenes, but kept himself in concealment, and was not rescued as so many captives were during the Quaker administration, but under an over-ruling providence, he was rescued at a later date, and brought to light under more propitious circumstances, when it became possible for him to become the liberator of the very people who had held him in captivity for so many years.

We will not repeat here the story of his recovery. But since the time of his realization of that greater recovery from superstition and idolatry of the Indian worship, through faith in Jesus Christ, his life has been given in an effort to free his captors from the captivity of sin and death.

As previously stated, he married Miss Emma McWhorter, daughter of the Rev. P.T. McWhorter, a most excellent helpmeet for him in all his work. They had no children, but they took into their home a number of children and trained them up to lives of usefulness, among whom was Rachel Downing, a beautiful and accomplished young woman, now the wife of Windell Briscoe. She is the granddaughter of Louis Downing, the noted Cherokee chief, who was a conspicuous character in the history of the Cherokee nation during and after the war between the states. In that tragic struggle he adhered to the union side. Another interesting character reared under their care is Mrs. Hattie Lang of Oklahoma City, formerly Hattie McKinzy. She is of the Kiowa tribe but of mixed Spanish blood. Both are Christians and faithful members of the Methodist church.

Andele had a large part in molding the character of others, both boys and girls, and little children cling to him wherever he goes, instinctively recognizing in him a friend.

A most excellent trait in the character of Andele is his purpose to reach the very highest standard in whatever he undertakes. When E-ton-bo took him into her care and began teaching him Indian songs and customs of the tribe, he made such rapid proficiency that it provoked other boys to envy, and they were disposed to treat him roughly, but being the adopted grandson of the chief, he held prestige on that account, and soon conquered a place of high standing in the tribe.

This aspiration to excel has remained with him through all the years and when he became a Christian, his effort has been to be the very best and most efficient Christian. Religion, therefore, has been to him a real experience, deep and definite.

From the time he knelt at the altar in the little mission church in "old Anadarko," many years ago, down to the present he has never faltered. In the face of opposition by the Indians and the ridicule of the frontier white man, he was, at first, somewhat troubled with a man-fearing spirit.

Telling of this one day, he said, "As you know, at the time of my conversion, I was working for the government at the old government sawmill. I had my bed in a room up over the sawmill. On account of this opposition, I felt much fear and shrinking, lest I should fail before it. One night after retiring, I could not sleep, and I lay there a long time troubling over this.

"At last I got out of bed and knelt down and asked God to help me to hold steady and not fear. Twice that night I did this before I could sleep, when the Lord answered my prayer, and all fear was gone, and never since that night have I had any fear of man, white or Indian."

Under the impress of the Holy Spirit, there was begotten in him a keen and delicate sense of discrimination and the fitness of things.

Soon after his conversion, he began work as industrial teacher in Methvin Institute, a Methodist Indian Mission school, and also as interpreter in the evangelistic field, although his English at this time was very crude. One day he said to me, "As you know, I used tobacco, but in this mission work, I came in contact with clean people. None of them used tobacco, but my body was saturated and my clothes stained with it. And when I rode with you in our work out among the Indians, as I smoke it would blow into your face. You made no protest, you said nothing. I felt condemned. I felt that it was not decent, nor Christlike. So I quit and was free." This was the summary statement of his tobacco experience.

The triumph of the gospel in his life, but demonstrates its power over the gripping force of superstition and idolatry as the following incident will show. It was in the summer of 1891.

We had been holding a meeting with the Indians under a brush arbor on Medicine Creek near the foot of Mt. Scott, which had continued for several days. At the close, we climbed to the summit of Mt. Scott to rest for a season, and to enjoy the scenery of the surrounding country. Sitting there upon a boulder on the mountain summit, he pointed out many places of interest, where in other days, wild and tragic scenes had been enacted. Finally, as he looked out towards Mt. Sheridan to the west, he said, "There in that depression to the west is where I crucified myself."

"What do you mean?" I asked.

He replied, "I will explain. How long back I know not, but for many, many years it has been the custom among the Indians for one who expects to achieve any great purpose in life to subject himself to certain forms of torture in worship. This he must do to find out his mission in life. I had great ambition to be a war-chief, and so I went there in that depression among the mountains, where I would be alone. I stripped and painted my body white. For four days and nights, without food or drink, I cried to the false gods of the Indians, and called upon my ancestors long since dead. I prodded my body with a sharp pointed instrument, and cut off bits of my skin and offered the skin and the blood to the sun, for we were both sun worshipers and ancestral worshipers. My body is now covered with scars where I mutilated myself in those wild days."

"Andele," said I, "will you show me those scars?"

"I am ashamed of it now," he replied, "but as we are here alone, I will show you." So he disrobed, and there in many places over his body were the lasting marks of his former superstitious worship. He said as he put on his clothes again, "In that feverish condition engendered by long fasting and torture, I seemed called to be a great medicine war-chief, but before I attained to any great efficiency either as a medicine man or war chief, I was rescued from the wild life, and you came with the gospel of truth and love, and the whole trend of my life was changed.

"Under a sense of God's pardoning love and redeeming grace, there came to me a keen sense of what was right and what was wrong, and what was real in religion and what was mere pretense. Even after my recovery to civilization, mere forms of religion which I witnessed seemed to be merely external, never reaching the heart and my soul's need. But when I heard the gospel from your lips, it seemed to penetrate my inmost soul, and it changed my whole life. I rejoice that you came, and now I realize the blessedness of His pardoning love and His redeeming grace."

It was a gracious hour that we spent there in the sunlight of that mountain top, and before we descended we knelt there together and poured out our souls in thanksgiving to our Heavenly Father for the unspeakable gift of his Son, and the consciousness of His pardoning love and redeeming grace.

As industrial teacher in Methvin Institute, he had charge of the boys in all their work, and, in harmony with the efforts of the teachers, he urged upon them a deep religious conviction.

In the evangelistic field he was indispensable and we depended much upon him. We traveled much together among the Indians, holding meetings out in the open under summer booths, or group meetings in their tepees in winter. Many were the conflicts we had and many were the victories won.

One evening, after a day of labor among the Comanches, we camped for the night on West Cache, south of the Wichita Mountains. The earth was parched and dry from long drought, the night was hot. Some distance down the creek, the sound of the tom-tom and the discordant hi-ya of the Indian song issuing from the medicine tepee came riding on the night wind. The multisonous yelping of a coyote, hungry and seeking food, added an occasional thrill to the scene, and gave emphasis to the night's experience. Myriads of mosquitoes, with their death song and their infectious sting, made a merciless attack upon us. We could not sleep, and all night long we fought them, trying every device to keep them off, till just before day, by covering my head in a blanket, I fell asleep in spite of the heat.

When I awoke the sun was up, but Andele was gone. I set out in search for him, and at last looking over the steep bank of the creek, he was discovered lying in a pool of water with just enough of his head on the sand bar, with face above water, to breath comfortably. Here, he found a secure refuge from the insects, and had a refreshing nap and comfortable bath; for the water was warm, the drought having continued so long that the creek had gone dry, except an occasional pool, here and there, in the channel, that under the continued heat was of about the temperature of the human body. In the old life that he had lived so many years, he had learned to take advantage of every device in emergencies.

From the time of his conversion on through the years that followed, such has been his devotion that gracious results have attended his efforts to save the Indians, and God has most wonderfully blessed his ministry.

One evening in a meeting on Medicine Creek near the foot of Mt. Scott, the Indians had been wrought up to an intense feeling. They were angry, and in the afternoon were grouped about here and there in threatening attitude. We had been ordered by some of them to hush. But that night in the face of the threat, I undertook to explain to the angry crowd some scripture appropriate to the occasion, Andele interpreting. But soon with the courage and inspiration born of the Spirit, he took the leadership in his own hands, and poured out upon them an exhortation of such pathos and power that the whole wild element came pressing to the front, and falling in the attitude of prayer and supplication, cried to God for mercy, while prayers and groans were heard throughout the camp. Many turned from the old way and started on the new, and all opposition for the time died.

Andele's perfect knowledge of the Indian languages and of all their customs and superstitions has all along given him access to them that others have not. And his perfect candor in dealing with them secures to him their utmost confidence.

They look to him for counsel and advice both in matters of religion and business, and hardly a day passes, and often many times a day, that some of them do not come to him for helpful counsel in their troubles. He has more influence among them than any other force either of church or state.

He has also a unique standing among the whites, and commands the respect and confidence of all.

Talking one day with a group of Christian friends concerning our labors in the ministry, I remarked that I had been defeated in so many ways in my work among the Indians and so much of it had been destroyed by designing hands, it seemed that I had wasted more than forty years of my life. One of the group replied, "No, no, there is Martínez." This intimation was sanctioned by all the group. They felt that it was worth all the years of labor and suffering to have been instrumental in leading him to Christ.

For years now, Andele, as a minister in the M.E. church, South, has been in charge of one of the Indian churches. Modest and unpretentious he delivers the message of salvation in simplicity and power, and at every service convictions are aroused and new life awakened in his hearers.

The sick (either physical or spiritual) among the Indians send for him far and near, and in his pastoral visitation, he cheers the sick and discouraged, and revives hope in the dying.

For a number of years, Andele lived upon his allotment of land and developed it to a high state of cultivation, and built upon it a neat country home. But later on he sold out everything and built a beautiful home in Anadarko where he now resides.

This change made it possible for him to give his whole time to the work of the ministry to which he has consecrated himself for life.

But this imperfect sketch of him must come to a close, and a fuller history reserved for the future.

He is now past his three score and ten years, but still erect and active, and with all the ardor of youthful enthusiasm in his efforts for the good of the people to whom he is called to minister.

For nearly forty years he and the writer have traveled and labored together, suffered privation and endured hardships, sleeping at night under the stars or in some Indian tepee, feasting at times on jerked beef or other crude diet served from the coals on willow switches or tin plates; but happy in it all as we urged upon them the saving truth of the gospel of the Son of God; and leaning upon each other, our hearts knit together in a blessed fellowship that must continue beyond the tomb.

Together we have seen the transformation of Indian life—from the nomadic life to settled homes; from the tepee to the neat well kept cottage; from the fantastic paraphernalia of the Indian dress, to the well regulated dress of civilization; from the crude diet of the old days, served upon the ground, to meals of well cooked food by skilled cooks on tables spread with snow white linen and served with the delicacy of refined and cultured homes; from the wild discordant worship of nature, to the peaceful worship of nature's God; from the medicine tepee with its nightly orgies, to the well built church houses with the inspiring melody of Christian song. And as we contemplate the changes we can but exclaim, "Behold what God has wrought!"

[The End]